SOFT FEET

Brian Nigus

Ordering Information

This book is available in a number of different formats,
including a limited edition signed version,
a print-on-demand paperback, digital formats for eReader devices,
and as a free PDF for reading, printing, and sharing.
For more information, visit the author's website at http://briannigus.com.

Publisher's Cataloging-in-Publication data

Nigus, Brian.
Soft Feet / Brian Nigus.
p. cm.
ISBN 978-0-9890718-1-9
1. History (Personal). 2. Memoir (Personal).
3. Reflection (Personal). 4. Travel Experience (Personal).
5. Sense (Philosophy). 6. Perception (Philosophy).

First Edition, print-on-demand paperback
10 9 8 7 6 5 4 3 2 1

Designed by Ryan Hageman.
Typeset in New Century Schoolbook and Super Grotesk.

For

Chris, Max, Rick, Sheri, Karen and Ken.

My brother, best friend, and all four parents.

And all of my families abroad.

Thank you.

CONTENTS

SOFT FEET

Soft Feet is a memoir. It is a collection of travel stories, starting from my childhood, and going until my most recent travels to Papua New Guinea. The narratives presented in this book are ones of my personal growth and transformation. Through hardships and adventures, they reveal insights and other life lessons that I hope others can relate to, or at the least, want to experience for themselves. These experiences have given me a greater awareness and appreciation for life, and it is my hope that their impact is contagious. Until one's feet have travelled outside of the home, one will never understand and appreciate the luxuries they rest upon.

Soft Feet starts with the assumption that we, Americans, are culturally inept in almost every regard.

> *This statement is obviously problematic. I try to stay away from generalizations, and even accusations, but if a book is going to take a side, some assumptions will have to be made. In this case, I am going to say that most people have soft feet, and when I say most people, I am specifically referring to Americans. Maybe even more specifically, white, middle-class, suburban Americans. But then again, I don't even think this provides a suitable capsule for my thoughts. In Carl Jung's case, he used "Europeans."*

Our comfort at home has caused our feet to atrophy, and turned our brains into insular minded mush. Industrialization and technology has removed us from our ancestral traditions without reciprocation, and we are confused with pride and feelings of non-privilege. America can be a big reclining chair that swallows you up, and keeps you sleeping for years, never letting your feet touch the ground to experience any discomfort or challenge. Even if we toured the many different places within the 49 readily road-trippable states, the ease of which to navigate the landscapes, towns, language, and customs is far too simple. This does nothing to harden our feet to the sharp thorn-laden ground that is our world. If we want to become better, sturdier representatives of our own country, we must venture past its borders and learn from Others. We must learn to walk on ground unfelt, and painful to our feet. Otherwise, our flabby feet will infect our legs and upward, turning our bodies and minds to Jell-O, easily swayed, and broken by the slightest glance.

To note, I am aware that every place in the United States of America has its own challenges and points of discomfort. These are good starting point experiences for those who are unable to find time or funds to travel too far from home, and from my own experience, are inspirational in their own right in creating sturdy representatives within the community close to home. If nothing else, one should seek discomfort, in order to better understand and define comfort.

This term *Soft Feet* comes from my two-month stay with the Sawiyano tribe inside the Wapualu Village of Papua New Guinea. The ground of the village was soft, but had rocks scattered throughout. The jungle paths were covered with thorns, broken sticks, and root systems. All the while, the tribe walked around barefoot, with the help of giant inch thick calluses that had formed on and around the pads of their feet. My shoes were constantly moist, and I soon became tired of wearing them. I started walking around barefoot, and quickly found out that my feet were much too soft, even for the village ground, and I had constantly to avoid the patches of rock. Over time though, my feet became hardened by the village floor and I walked comfortably wherever I went. I even took short walks into the jungle bush, reminding me of my childhood when we played barefoot outside, acorns resting on the ground in the most inopportune spots, causing my legs to unexpectedly buckle under the sharp pain. My feet had acquired newfound strength, and aside from the several thorns I received, I no longer flinched when I stepped onto broken twigs or sharp stones. Traveling to new places does this for our bodies and minds. It strengthens us.

When thinking about this term, it is important that hardened feet is not confused with numb feet. Nothing is maybe worse than having no feelings at all, and feet will only become numb when they are no longer used. Even the tribe members stepped upon painful thorns that I had to help pull out, albeit the size of their thorns being five times the size of one that would paralyze me. We must feel the ground, and we must be open to new feeling, experiencing the ground of Others so that we may better walk on our own. If we simply walk without feeling, we are not truly walking. Benjamin Franklin wrote:

> *"Like a man traveling in foggy weather, those at some distance before him on the road he sees wrapped up*

in the fog, as well as those behind him, and also the
people in the fields on each side, but near him all
appears clear, tho' in truth he is as much in the fog
as any of them."

We must harden our feet, but never lose their ability to feel, or their means of which to change direction, during this journey on the interconnected earth road.

Soft Feet is a recollection of experiences that I feel have developed my own soles and perspective. I write from specific travels, sharing stories and revealing insights from my past participation and walking.

Franco la Cecla tributes Eva Serra for saying:

"One writes books to find a way of making sense of the
years one has just lived through."

While Carl Jung states:

"I am not a critic ... I am trying to understand. Many
things which might displease me will no longer
displease me when I understand what their cause is."

Writing helps me to understand, and continued travel keeps these understandings in question (as concrete answers are soon crumbled, and comfy couches are soon made uncomfortable with dents from where you slumbered). Maybe like David Abram, I am disappointed and confused in regards to how little we participate with this world, and the distress to which our interdependencies have had to endure. The endless man-madeness that we exist in has trapped us into comfort and complacency. Fear of dangers beyond our control, and codes to which we must live up to deter us from taking risks and limit our exploration and innovation. We are stuck in trying to create right angles after right angles, despite their impossibility. We blindly move around, but only because we choose to keep our eyes closed.

Our vision is blurred, and we are privileged enough to choose what we want to see. For at some point, the interdependencies of relation-ships seem farther removed than others. The question naturally becomes then, one of editing, or prioritizing which relations we must place importance on, (maybe especially in a time when technology gives us a pseudo-sense of world-wide participation). With the breakdown of communication between ourselves and the earth, so comes the breakdown of our own communication with each Other. We lack the ability to create meaningful relationships with other humans, due to our lacking relationship with the earth. We must access new thought processes, and we must strive to walk on new ground constantly.

I recognize that I am extremely fortunate and privileged to have traveled as far from home as I have, and while I know that these journeys aren't possible for everyone, I hope to bring some sort of relevance through provoked conceptions of every day life that are possible in any context. You will be able to tell through my anecdotes and voice that I was born into a life of privilege, but it is my hope that this collection of writing starts to fulfill the responsibility that a privileged person has in giving back to a world that so generously raised him. Soft Feet attempts to inspire active curiosity and progression, bring awareness to new ideas, and encourage new ways of thinking and doing.

Benjamin Franklin once wrote, "Common sense aided by present danger, will sometimes be too strong for whimsical opinions." I came upon this quote during my trip to Papua New Guinea, and think it is appropriate as a cautionary statement for a book filled with my own whimsical opinions. While I have left out certain pages that sound more like complaints, I have kept a majority that I hope can be insightful or thought-provoking as such a whimsical state that reading allows. I also think that this quote is a strong caveat for students who are trained, or are training in making opinions about a society, or world, and due to lack of experience, are left to these means only. It might make more sense then to say, "Whimsical opinions are strong when similar common sense aided by similar present danger have been experienced." I hope there is something interesting in this book for everyone.

> *"The meaning of a book is given, in the first instance, not so much by its ideas as by a systematic and unexpected variation of the modes of language, or narrative, or of existing literary forms. This accent, this particular modulation of speech—if the expression is successful—is assimilated little by little by the reader, and it gives him access to a thought to which he was until then indifferent or even opposed."*

> — *Maurice Merleau-Ponty*

FOREWORD / THANKS

Geographical displacement is a central part of both my process and the content of this work. The exploratory nature of travel, especially trips to a new landscape or culture, triggers a stimulation of all senses. This sudden confusion is an excellent device for achieving a more conscious and considerate engagement with both society and self. The potential for memory to morph and add meaning to events that are temporal, yet significant, is important when creating new works. This book documents my experience and reflections regarding my time spent abroad, in relation to my time spent at home, and other ideas regarding humanity.

There are many people that have made this book possible, and all the more worthwhile, through financial support, and continued conversations leading up to it. While I find this reminiscent of high school yearbook signings, I don't think there are enough books that start off with thank yous.

My brother, Chris Nigus, has been there for me since I can remember. From the whiny days of my youth, I still remember the time he gave me twenty-five cents to get something from one of the grocery store "junk machines." I remember the time he traded me Slurpees after we had crossed Antioch Road and mine had slipped out of my hands all over the ground. I remember all of the events that led him to be my student loan cosigner. And I remember the road trips and adventures we took together after his graduation from the Naval Academy. But the one thing I don't remember, which is something he loves to tell, is the time he threw a ball and broke the glass window in our house. When dad came home, it was blamed on me, and I got the biggest ass-whoopin' he had ever seen. So Chris, be glad I don't remember that. I love you. Thank you for all of your continued support.

My parents, Karen Huffman and Rick Nigus, did an amazing job raising me. Simply stated, I know life before I left for college was difficult, but it's easy to tell that there's a reason outside of luck and hard work that I'm where I am today. As I enter the years of adulthood, I can start to imagine the sacrifices that must be made when a child is born. Thank you for putting food on the table every night, even when I wouldn't eat your beef-mushroom-gravy concoction. Thank you for signing me up for school and making sure I had all the tools to succeed, including the deluxe 256-count Crayola crayon set with built-in crayon sharpener. And thank you for challenging me every step of the way, keeping me accountable for all of my actions.

My step-parents, Sheri Rowen-Nigus and Ken Huffman, not only show love and compassion to me, but they also do a mighty fine job of loving my parents. I hope you continue to hold hands with them in public for many years to come!

My best friend, Max Grove, taught me how to be patient and fall asleep to the sound of snores that were reminiscent of helicopter takeoffs and landings. More importantly, we know each other's tolerances and deepest secrets through Guinness dinners, and two-for-ones right before classes at art school. Thank you for having the same sense of humor as me, and inspiring me to take more risks.

My friends Jenny Bookler, Katy Vonk, Mel Nguyen, Eric Frye, Maura Doyle and Erin Hael have continued to have conversations with me after college. They helped me realize that trying to place art on Maslow's hierarchy was ill-advised, and that if I continued trying, I would start placing my friends on there as well, falsifying in my mind, the indefinite truth that we all need each other for survival.

My friend, Ryan Hageman has inspired me through his own steadfast beliefs on world justice, and care. His committed studies of Japanese culture and language have encouraged me to follow my own interests without regard for expected, or immediate outcomes. He is also responsible for the design of this book.

My professors Kinji Akagawa and Ruth Voights have instilled in me a great sense of care for the world. Ruth's lessons on ecology, myth, ritual, space, and place triggered a deeper concern for what I couldn't perceive. In turn, Kinji's participation for perception, and other life lessons that many can attest to, have kept me on a path for empathy and love. I challenge myself to have an even bigger smile than either of them someday. Thank you for the lessons.

Last, but not least, I would like to thank Bethany Kalk for inviting me to partake in her trip to Papua New Guinea. Bethany was a previous professor of mine, but it wasn't until I met one of her colleagues that I was reconnected with her via Facebook.

"Hey Brian,

(...) if you have your next summer open...

I just wanted to let you know that I am going to Papua New Guinea (where I grew up) Summer 2012. So if you are looking for a different kind of trip, you are welcome to come."

Now that the trip has passed, I can't even start to thank her for the opportunity she gave me. The tribe we lived with became a strong family for me, and I learned more than I could have possibly imagined. Thank you Bethany.

This book, as well as my trip to Papua New Guinea, was funded by many of my friends through Kickstarter, a website dedicated to launching small business and individual projects. In addition to the many thank you notes already sent out, I would like to again, thank all 86 of the people who helped make this project possible for me. Thank you! And thank you for having shared this project with your friends and family. 21 people I have never met donated this way! As a full time pizza delivery driver, artist, gardener, after school teacher, and gallery assistant working an average of 80 hours per week at the time of raising funds, it was impossible to push this project along by myself. Thank you. Supporters of this project include, but are not limited to:

Teresa Audet

Jenny Bookler

Christopher Bowman

Kermit Boyum

Susan Calmenson

Kathy Daniels

Meg Dolan

Ken and Ingrid Douglas

Daphne Eck and
    Caleb Coppock

Darlene Fuhst and
    JJ Ohlinger

Rev. Maxwell W. Grove

Ryan Hageman

Ash Marlene Hane

Karen and Ken Huffman

Brad P. Jirka

Hannah Kleese

Megan Leafblad and
    Michael Gottschalk

You You Mi

Kerry Morgan

Chris Nigus

Rick and Sheri Nigus

Sepik Pikinini

Ms. Lee Alani Selvey

Emily Sheehan

Erin Standley

Marci Ann Watkins

Karen Wirth

A HISTORY OF STORIES / INTRODUCTION TO THE INTEREST

These stories recount my adventures and happenings that have led to, what I consider, the importance of geographical displacement, experience and reflection. While I plan on future adventures, it is my hope to continue regarding our space, place, and interdependent relationships with the infinite others in this life-world. A tool for reflection and empathy.

> We must trust ourselves to be true and honest when looking into ourselves, knowing full well that what we do is "repetitious" of history, but new and good for the self. While at the same time, we should not disregard the thoughtfulness and care of other thinkers who have these understandings. Whether atrocious or wonderful, history is "repeated," and in doing so we edge closer to a fuller understanding of how to perceive such things. Since we can never gain a complete empathy due to the innate variable of our self and its accumulated past, this then leads to the question of whether "repetition" is useful.
>
> "I hate traveling and explorers. Yet here I am proposing to tell the story of my expeditions."
>
> — Claude Lévi-Strauss, Tristes Tropiques

*"To explain is not to present a set of finished reasons,
but to tell a story."*

— David Abram

Apparently, when I was just a baby, my parents would travel around the United States in my dad's blue Aerostar mini-van. These memories are only known to me because of my brother having told me. My dad had removed the backseat benches of the van in order to create a makeshift bed out of plywood. Underneath this bed, my family stored our supplies, from clothes and food, to fishing gear. My brother tells me that we sat together on the bed while my mom and dad sat in the front seats. No seat belts to keep us safe, we were left to wiggle around freely and play card games, or hit each other, as my dad drove the usual 90 miles per hour along the interstate, only once getting pulled over. What is strange to me, from the fragments of these memories, were the places and objects that interrupted the van rides.

Small tokens, souvenirs, rest stops, nature, objects/experiences that caught my attention and created memory of places are things that when I reflect on, and see pictures of, seem to have torn me away from wrestling with my brother. The ability for a restroom break, or an adventure around the surrounding landscape as mom and dad switched front seats, or a small stuffed animal parrot that I named Bill to bring a smile to my face is intriguing. For all of the pictures my family has kept (or at least shows to the public), are all ones of me smiling, and yet, I only remember being a brat.

Maybe it was just me getting my way with the stuffed parrot, but outside of these objects that possessed my affection and care, the landscape itself seemed to also possess me. I like to joke that this is only because I was finally able to slow down and kiss the earth after having traveled 90 miles an hour inside of a metal box for hours on end. This extreme contrast of weaving through highway traffic, to standing still amongst a forest of trees might well have added to my mood change, but I think the newness, or introduction of new perceptions may have played an even greater role. Every time the van stopped, it was like a time machine had taken us to a new landscape two hours into the future. In fact, I guess, this is exactly what it was doing. Each exit from the vehicle activated my senses with new smells, sounds, sights, and feelings. I was no longer occupied by the narrowness and familiarity of our traveling time-machine. I was opened up to unfamiliarity, and awakened to adventure.

This sense of adventure continued during my stay at 7315 Dearborn, the first home I remember growing up in. More specifically, this sense, or intimate relationship with the ground, continued up the street at my best childhood friend's house. His name is Joe Cowan.

Children have the amazing privilege of free time and exploration, one that adults tend to leave behind due to what we might call "responsibility." And while some adults may meld their free time into their responsibilities better than others, children need not even try, as most children are consumed by the responsibilities of their imagination. Playing outside, running around, scraping dirt, inventing games, hide and seek, looking for bugs under rocks, peeing into the neighbor's garden, and jumping on trampolines. While this may be a short-sighted view of the privileged childhood I experienced, I would like to think that there is an innate difference between children and adults, regarding their relationships to the world, whichever corner of the globe they inhabit. The fact here being, Joe and I were active explorers of our neighborhood world.

I remember the routine quite clearly. Whether it was the school year or the summer, wake up, get home, whatever the case being, the objective was to head up the street towards Joe's house and see if he could come outside to play. There were three options usually. Ride bikes between the neighbor's driveways while trying to perform the biggest wheelies we could, jump on his trampoline from our improvised tree house despite my own mother's warnings, or looking for bugs under rocks and putting them into jars with hole-punched lids. We almost always looked for bugs.

I don't quite remember, nor can I assume the origin of this activity, but whatever we started with each day, we always found ourselves going back to the bug hunt. Lifting boulders to reveal underground homes, scattering its inhabitants throughout the backyard, and causing a chase. We were monsters in a way, but we were also curious and active in our outside world. We tore up the concrete patio and dug around its edges, we scraped the dirt around the trees, and we especially liked the side of the house where the slugs tended to congregate after heavy rainfalls. And yes, I have to admit, that we did in fact sprinkle salt onto a couple of slugs, an activity that was short lived as we were much more keen on keeping the slugs alive to creep out his younger sisters. The sense of discovery, capture, and release held presence over our activity.

On Summer nights, when the air was just right, there were amazing performances of lightning bugs that we would chase throughout the yard and put into our jars. We would bring them into the garage and turn off the lights in order to watch their abdomens light up. The subtle hum of on and off glowing around the space was captivating. The lightning bugs were special, in the sense that they dazzled us with lights shows, and were also the only creatures we found who had the ability to climb out of our jars. We found this out the hard way as we fell asleep with our jars in the living room, and found them to be empty the next morning as we woke to the screams of Joe's sisters. Since youth, I can't remember one night where the lightning bugs returned to our neighborhood for their light display. Whether from my own blindness, or our world's decreasing health, I cannot remember one sighting thereafter.

Joe and I eventually upgraded to an old aquarium that we used to house the different captured bugs. We added dirt, rocks, sticks and leaves, and little pieces of leftover lunch snacks to create what we thought would be a great environment. We spent hours in the backyard in hundred degree weather, finding bugs, running them to the aquarium, finding more bugs, and so on. This became our routine. Sadly, the bugs all died. We were not suitable homemakers for them, and we suspected that the nightcrawler had devoured them all, as it was the only one left over when we emptied the aquarium.

These bug hunts continued for summers on end, but became severely interrupted when video games entered into our lives. We became crippled to the couch, and it soon became a punishment to play outdoors. Joe's mother would make us stay outside for at least an hour before we could return to Sonic the Hedgehog. In essence, we left our bug-hunting world behind, as well as our intimate relationship with the ground. A relationship that used to pull us with ease, like gravity over our bodies to the earth, but now seemed less exciting in comparison to this new human-made magic.

What bothers me about this story, is what I assume most children today must be facing. I was introduced to technology after having explored the outside, and while I know these gaming systems were available before this, the ease and accessibility of these complex virtual realms are now in abundance. Are kids these days allowed the opportunities of outside, before being bombarded with the infection of technology? Even with cartoon mascots that encourage you to exercise and play outside, they are still embedded in technology, and the messages tend to fall on deaf ears. From my own experience of working with young students in schools, there is a definite lack of outdoor activity, despite their abundance of energy. There are even gym teachers that I have met who use televisions to show workout videos in their classes. This is an activity that only solidifies the eye's gaze, and detaches it from the bodily movements that are performed. A message that says these exercises are important for your body, but can only be heard through this screen. To turn your head away, is to fail the exercise. Even web-cam projectors used in the classroom captivate students in this way, as they project virtual images of humanness through a type of "screen." And yet, it seems, this is the result we have succumbed to as students faced with activities outside are too distracted and unable to "perform" the desired actions. There is no captivating screen to hold their gaze. What do they turn to then? They turn to talking with their friends, joking about yesterday's basketball game, running around, and some even pull the homework from their backpacks to get a head start on free time at home. Aren't these good things? Socializing, exercising, self-directed learning, and yet, we have a hard time with them because they are not part of the plan, or under our control as teachers. This desire for control not only grows out of our culture's expectations of respect for elders, but it is also a consequence of our society's desire to make every student "up to par." While there are economical punishments for teachers, and whole schools who cannot "make" their students meet a national average, there is an even greater social punishment caused by these school systems that do "make" their students meet a national average.

Suppose a high school is threatened with losing accreditation due to its standardized test score results. The school also hosts a large number of disabled and English as a secondary language students, all of which have to meet this national quota. With standards that don't accommodate for diverse populations, this not only creates a tension between students and teachers, but also students and students. Assumptions and racism are felt throughout the hallways, and the only thing a school like this can do to alleviate the pressure is to cheat. Some teachers work through the tests with classes, allow talking during the tests, and make sure the students score above average. The teachers are allowed to keep their jobs, and in some cases, even get bonuses. In the meantime, the school looks good on paper for accreditation purposes.

Though, we can't cheat, or conform to standards forever. We have to find a new way of learning. A way of learning that is in unison with that exploration of our past. (Especially if we think that it is important that our country be competitive in this idea of progress, a term that needs to be reconsidered itself, as we continually digress in regards to our relationships with Others.) We need to develop a new way of learning and activeness.

As a "gifted" student, I participated in weekly independent studies. I now recognize though, that there were still problems to this freedom of exploration I was given. I was never detached from the idea of needing to get good grades, and there was the assumption that if I did well, I would be picked up and recognized, without any of my own intervention after the fact of my workings. This ludicrous idea led me down the path of an assignment based life, doing things simply to do them, in hopes of some sort of return, i.e. scholarship, job offer, celebrity status.

The desired result was one of a so-called, comfortable life. Free from working hard. If I worked hard now, I wouldn't have to work hard later. This is the idea we teach our students, as if there is no other way to enforce hard work without the reward of a future that doesn't need it. A shame, because now, more than ever, we need hard workers. This can't be done through test scores, cheated results, or even complete freedom (for once we are introduced to structure, we become lost without it, and must be weaned into a life of freedom and productive self-direction). Maybe through examples of our own lives being lived, can students pick up on these values. Maybe through a restructured curriculum that throws us off of the current dilapidated ballasts and moves towards self-direction. And while I can't provide concrete solutions, maybe a reflection of one's own past can help provide insight, and a closer grasp on empathy for students' present needs as they work towards their future, full of Others.

As I grew older, and moved into the front seat of cars, this feeling of unfamiliar space revelations changed. Unlike my past position of backseat baby, I was now able to pay attention to the surrounding space we were travelling through. Whenever we stopped, I had already had time to survey the land through the van's windshield. I would no longer be able to exit into an unfamiliar landscape for I had already assumed and concluded what was around me. It wasn't until I took my first flight alone that I remember feeling this sort of excitement and reawakening of senses.

My best friend at the time, Matt Straus, was moving to Myrtle Beach, South Carolina, far away from our hometown suburbia of Overland Park, Kansas. I don't remember asking if I could go visit him, but I think my parents, who were then just recently divorced, must have thought it would be a good idea for me to see him. I was thirteen years old, had just finished 7th grade, and airports were still skittish from the previous September. My mom escorted me through the Kansas City International airport and watched me walk through the gate. For those who have travelled through the Mid-Continent International airport, you know that it is one of the easiest to navigate airports in the country. You walk in and the gates are right there in front of you, just behind a glass wall. Check your bags, turn, and there's your gate, each with its own security check. And if your friends sending you off would like to stay and write messages on pads of paper to communicate with you before your flight boards, that's perfectly fine. The bullet-proof glass walls allow for this.

My mom had some sort of appointment that day though, and while she saw me to the point of finding a seat behind the glass and become comfortable with my CD-player, she was off. For the first time, I was alone and overwhelmed by a surrounding of unfamiliarity. Something was different though, different than those past unfamiliar situations that were calming and full of curiosity. Although I might not have shown it, this newness started to become full of anxiety. For two hours I watched the businessmen with their state-of-the-art, oh-so-chunky laptops, the families that sat together opening up their pre-made trip-snacks reminiscent of my own family's past excursions, the TV monitors displaying news from the war, and the omniscient clock with it's built in drone voice, announcing the boarding times of every gate.

Eventually, my flight boarded, and since I was a young person travelling by myself, they allowed me to board first. I was worried that my sweat had ruined the ticket's validity, but it worked just fine. I was assured by all of the staff and flight attendants that I would enjoy the flight, and if I needed any help, they would assist me. I had become pretty quiet with adults after my parent's divorce, so I just nodded and followed the path to my seat. After all, this was my second flight, and the process itself wasn't wholly unfamiliar. I knew the feeling of entering the long tube-like chamber with it's far-too-fresh-to-be-real air being pumped into it. I knew how it felt to be thrown back into my chair as the thrusters came on at take-off, and I even knew the gum trick so that I could pop my ears accordingly. There was another challenge to overcome though, and that was my transfer in Atlanta.

First time flyers can attest to the nervousness of transferring alone. Even veteran flyers, in foreign airports, can expect to have this sense of confusion. At age thirteen, I remember walking out of the gate and being bombarded by the most densely packed human traffic I had ever experienced. I kind of followed everyone else, hoping they would lead me to the departure board, as my mom had advised. I couldn't see anything, as almost everyone else was two feet taller than me, and so I had to wait until it cleared out.

I remember that my gate was within some other terminal of the airport, and whether it was nervousness, or an oversight, I couldn't tell where to go. I walked straight to the nearest desk and asked where my gate was. They told me to just keep walking straight. For those who have flown through the Atlanta airport, they know that it is probably the second most easy to navigate, and thus, most likely, a nerve-induced oversight on my part.

The walk was simple and long, but I can still feel the emptiness of the great open air-hallways. I had not experienced this architectural strategy before, and it was amplified even more so by my tiny, yet chubby, frame (I prefer the term husky). My neck was like an owl's, rotating to take in every sensation that was coming at me. It was amazing.

I felt a rush of pride and success as I reached my gate, and confirmed with the staff member at the desk that this was where I needed to be. From then on, I was an expert traveler, and I wanted more!

> *To note, after recalling this story with my friend Matt, he brought to my attention that we had driven to South Carolina, and I flew back to Kansas City. Virtually, a complete reversal of the story I just told. Intriguing, because this means that the whole first half, regarding my mom, is a complete lie. While she has dropped me off many times to the airport, this event, in its context, never happened, and brings me back to this idea that, "the potential for memory to*

morph and add meaning to events that are temporal, yet significant, is important." For me, it's not exactly a lie, as it is a mis-memory, a memory that has been pieced together from past events, (actual or non-actual) and presented as an honest perception. This is in no way a complete fabrication of, or an attempt to create a new personal mythology (such like Joseph Beuys or Jay-Z, if I can put them into the same sentence), but instead, a recollection of something I truly believe to have happened.

So then, is truth important with regard to stories like this? Or is it more important to believe in our own primary perceptions and speak from them? To build our own truth? Or just to grow from feeling and realize what is important to us, whether true or not?

A caveat here is that the word perception is not to be confused with presumption, which is a "thing that is accepted as true or as certain to happen, without proof," whereas perception is, "our ability to see, hear, or become aware of things through the senses."

So we may be able to presume things to happen because we don't require proof, but we are unable to ever presume a perception, due to its innate need for sensory participation. Perception requires participation (Maurice Merleau-Ponty). And as no moment is ever the same, neither are our perceptions during these moments. A child sitting in the front seat of a car going 70 miles per hour may hide in fear, as the speed they are experiencing is perceived as much faster than the perceptions that the adult driver is having. Even a raised voice can sound like yelling from the scale of a child. We can't just isolate these perceptions to single moments though, for the accumulation of the day, the week, and our lives affects each present moment. We perceive each moment differently and these perceptions serve as our primary, or personal, truths. But then, is it important for us to clarify between a perception we know to be true, and a perception we feel to have been true? Is there a difference? The revelation of process that happens after looking at a photograph and realizing that it is indeed a physical set out in the world, and not simply two images juxtaposed together on the computer can affect your original perception. But would it have mattered if you had known otherwise? How you first perceive something is the foundation from which you experience it.

I'm going to side with the idea that as long as you don't know you're lying, it is important to always be honest. To be aware of a falsity, and to go forward with it, invites more trouble, while being unaware of your lies (or at least delusional of them) invites education and active learning if you are open to being corrected (if society demands there is the need for it). This reminds us of Mike Daisey, a professional actor and storyteller who is one of the biggest enemies of the Apple Corporation. While monologuing on Foxconn, a company he visited in that produces Apple parts, he over exaggerates excruciating conditions and employs storytelling devices that create outrage in the audience against Apple, as well as a whole nation. While his falsities were brought to light, Daisey holds onto some of them as truths, in the sense that they were his perceptions during the visit, how he felt them to be. Aside from the fact that actors' jobs are to convince others of something that is not true, Daisey's performance hit a road bump as it aired on "This American Life," a radio talk show founded on truth, not perceptions or feelings.

Being aware of your lies doesn't always cause harm though. Like the artist Joseph Beuys, contemporary rapper Jay-Z also fabricated his personal mythology. Are we truly supposed to believe that he was shot at point-blank while each bullet missed him? No one is silly enough to think that this is actually true. But, does believing this story hurt anyone, or is it simply a tool for Jay-Z to elevate himself and build a self-confidence that he couldn't do otherwise? This talk attempts to give him god-like status and in doing so, even portrays his own divulgence of the luck that one requires to gain celebrity status.

We all create personal mythologies for ourselves that we end up believing, and as time goes on, these beliefs become even more rooted and skewed as we lose sight of the original experience, or perception. While we are defined by each other, we are also attached to our own individual definitions (and our intentions) of our perceptions. It might be a contradiction in itself (in the sense that all perceptions are participatory), but I refer to these as personal, or primary perceptions, as they are the ways in which we ourselves see and understand the events that unfold in our lives, before Others have the chance to reveal their own understandings. For if everyone sees events in a different light, how do we differentiate truths from lies? And then the other question is, what actually happens in the world if we all perceive things differently? And since we cannot see every possible angle, how very important then, is our interdependency? These thoughts led me to certain projects like the wagon racer, and sensing glasses. Both were tools to experience the moment where life flashes before your eyes, and the other of being blind. Does this yearning for insight from other perspectives neglect my own, or does it add more awareness to a collective perception?

These personal mythologies are not necessarily induced by ourselves. Society tells us to create our stories. We innately compare ourselves to others and believe in the amazing things that Others do. As we watch interviews, society seeks the answers to how celebrities turned out to be who they are. What makes you you? We then search for these answers for ourselves and come up with skewed reasons that slow down our present nature, as if we must continue to fit in with what we think we are being.

Victor Hunt does this in his DesignArt Documentaries where he talks to emerging designers and their past. During an interview, he has Kwangho Lee reflect on his childhood and describe how he came to the present. Lee eventually says, "When I was younger, I lived on a farm. At the beginning, I was actually just doing my work, and did not quite realize what I was experiencing. I find myself to be influenced more and more by what I felt then." While not malicious, the idea that he grew up a farmer is preposterous. If anything, he grew up a designer, playing a farmer. While the tulip grows up from its bulb in the ground, it is rooted at its base. It experiences everything around it, and may in fact grow in many different places, but it will always sense and perceive the world as a tulip. Only upon reflection and looking upon itself and other tulips, does it realize that it is only a tulip. This is good, and it is imperative to know and understand.

This question of harm then is a bit tricky, because while a personal mythos may be small and useless outside of promoting the self, an institutional mythos, much like the ones that American colleges employ today, can be devastating. Creating an amplified image and purporting fantastical futures not only traps students into financial debts, but also facilitates the upkeep of celebrities in the system that the college supports. Did Marcel Duchamp realize what he was doing when he started everyone talking? Maybe it does fall into his paradox interests, but it seems that this action has grown into whole buildings dedicated to simply talking about art in order to fund its existence through student debt. Institutions like these need to take care to see if they are creating an illusionist trap for their consumers to fall into, or if they are themselves delusional of what they think their consumers need, and whether or not they can change.

In conclusion of this digression, be aware that these stories may be tainted with little memory synapses that have connected onto other memory synapses, in order to create falsities I am unaware of. I don't mean to induce any harm, just to recall what I believe to be personal accounts that have turned me into who I am today. I will not tell you that I "was promptly rescued by a nomadic tribe of Tartars, who saved (my) life by greasing (my) bruised and battle-weary body with animal fat, before wrapping (me) entirely— so as to raise (my) temperature—in felt." Though, that's one heck of a story.

"A little bit of lying is ok."

-Kinji Akagawa

My first deep encounter with nature is also connected to my most embarrassing moment. As a wee sprout, I was full of pride.

Growing up, I remember that my family would take big trips to various places around town. As we all lived in or around Kansas City, it was easy enough to meet up. My cousins, aunts, uncles and grandparents would all be there. We would put on our best new outfits and impress each other with how well we were all doing. For the kids, it was a time to get to know each other and hang out. I have to assume that for the adults, it was also a time to catch up and see how life was faring.

For one of these trips, we decided to go to the Kansas City Zoo, which still survives and is worth a visit if you're ever in town. I was wearing my new top-of-the-line Bugs Bunny hooded t-shirt combination, with my new jean shorts. I was the epitome of 90s child fashion, and in fact, my aunt came to think that I loved clothes so much that instead of buying me the normal boy-targeted gift cards, she bought me gift cards to fashion outlets.

I was extremely excited about this day-long journey to the zoo and was ready to explore. Despite it being one of the farthest destinations from the entrance, I made it very clear that the lion's cage was where I wanted to go first. I was assured that we would get there in time, but I demanded the lions! They were my favorite animal, the character of one of my favorite animations, and what I wanted more than anything else. So I cried and whined until eventually my family gave in. As it so happened, the sea-lions (who ironically just happened to have their homes next to the lion-lions) were having a show, and if we left then, we could split up and all be happy.

We ran to the other side of the park and I was so excited to be seeing my favorite animal. I was entranced by the whole arrangement of it all. A huge concrete stage laid in front of a perimeter of steel bars that, if one dared to do so, could step upon, walk towards the cage, and actually reach out to touch the lion if it came close enough. I stood with my face next to the bars, excited and scared, watching the lions sleep. Soon enough, one of the lions was awakened by my presence, and I could see its huge jaws open into a long yawn. It stretched its muscles and seemed to be going through a sort of routine like my dad might, shaking his head and arms as if trying to rotate some life into his joints that had just been immobilized for 8 hours. The male lion made his way into a slumbered walk and slowly paced within the caged environment. He was lethargic. His predatory instincts and courage seemed to have been traded in for a lack of ambition and helplessness. With this in mind, the beast met eyes with me and slowly approached my location. Nothing was fazing me, for I was about to see every detail of my favorite animal. From the tufts of his mane, to his giant padded paws, I felt compelled to pet him, albeit my being frozen by his sheer mass. The king walked back and forth in front of me and then stopped. He seemed to slowly walk back towards where he had left his body-print just moments before. Instead, he simply kicked the ground with one hind leg and backed up towards the cage bars like some sort of delivery truck into a loading dock. And with the divine swing of a brand new cabinet door, his tail shot straight up and a fist-sized stream of piss shot all over me! There was no escape from this jet-powered hose of urine. I staggered straight back. It seemed unending. My brother and cousins tell me that it must have been a distance of at least twenty feet. And the stream never died down, it just simply shut off, as if the monster had an on/off pee switch. I'm positive that every last drop had been released onto my Bugs Bunny hooded t-shirt and new jean shorts.

I was drenched in a yellow liquid that myths and legends could describe as a holy blessing that induced magical powers, only in this case, the fantastic was much more mundane. I smelled like lion piss. I was the laugh of the crowd, and if only YouTube had been invented, I might now be a star. I don't remember too much after my first and only interspecies golden shower experience, but afterwards, we joked that I had gotten the best souvenir out of any of the visitors that day, a bag full of urine-drenched clothes, and a free towel to walk around naked in for the day. Seriously, who actually *gets* permission to walk around naked for the day? I can't say I had this foresight back then, as I must have been pretty heated, but long story short, I think nowadays I prefer to be patient, rather than pissed.

The introduction of architecture, home, and space in general, came during my Summer stay in The Netherlands. After having finished my studies in Ireland, I continued on to the harbor city of Rotterdam, full of interesting post-war architecture, rolled up sleeves and the color orange. Before arriving, I had done great research in finding an apartment for my three-month stay. Through an online service, I met a lady named Mary, and she had a room within one of her properties available for rent. It was in my price range, and after having had several discussions with her regarding the local art scene, and having filled out a housing contract, I sent her my security deposit and first month's rent. To make this short and sweet, she (or he) stole all of that money and discontinued all conversation with me. It turned out that I was involved in one of many housing scams, and I now had $23 to my name.

I called the studio that I was going to be working for and explained that I couldn't afford to come. More so, I explained that I needed a place to stay because my return ticket to America wasn't for another 4 months. As many travelers know, changing the date of your ticket can cost just as much as the original ticket itself. I was in no position for this option, and unwilling to test the generosity of the airlines. After talking with the studio, they were in good spirits with me, telling me that they would help me find a place to stay for cheap, if not free. As well, they would give me an advance of pay so I could stay afloat. Since squatting is legal in The Netherlands, they thought they would help me find a space in town. There was no such luck. I was told to come to the studio anyway and we would figure it out.

I arrived in Rotterdam from Ireland, and took a taxi to the studio with what little I had left. The cab driver was confused as the address I gave him actually happened to be in the harbor. Although I knew that the studio rested on the harbor's edge, I was also confused because I had never been to the space. We eventually found the right warehouse and he dropped me off. Like a true Rotterdammer, the taxi driver asked if I was sure I would be ok before leaving. Yes, it's true, every person I met in Rotterdam was nice, including the guy who tried to sell me a gun at the sports bar while I was talking to my mom on video chat.

The large green gate to the property was opened, and I walked into the yard of the studio. This consisted of stacked shipping containers, fiber glass sculptures, a few flat bed trailers, a door that led into changing rooms, a large staircase going up to an office and top-floor lounge, and then a huge open garage door that led into the fabrication shop. I walked in and found two very interesting men, smoking and welding at the same time. A sense of freedom from the rules and regulations of my university's fabrication shop was easily brought to my attention. They looked up and I introduced myself. "Ah! You must be the new intern! We heard all about how you lost your money. We've been making fun of you all week!" Embarrassed, they continued to introduce themselves and show me around the shop. It was huge! Fully equipped fiber glass, metal, and wood sections all in one large sectioned off space. Afterwards, they showed me where I would be staying.

One of the two gentlemen had been living in the harbor for 8 years by this time, and he had the wonderful idea of having me sleep in the shipping container beneath him. I laughed, but thought well, as long as the doors lock, I'll be ok. I had my backpack, three changes of clothes, my camera and my laptop. Sure enough, the doors worked just fine, and we grabbed a mattress to complete the scene. I had just left one of the most beautiful Irish landscapes, and traded it for a lonely, grungy harbor in Rotterdam. Even though I had shelter, and never once slept on the street, I felt close to homeless.

This feeling was only amplified due to the context of my previous Irish cottage space.

My space was small and empty. It was a big steel box. It got cool at night, and hot in the day time. You could smell the resin and chemicals from the studio, and two flies constantly buzzed around the box, a sound that bounced off of the metal ever so softly throughout the night. I felt safe, albeit the shady rendezvous happenings in the harbor's cul-de-sac just outside my box. Some nights I could hear people in the yard, and I didn't want to look out. After having learned how to be free and wild with my many friends in Ireland, I learned the lessons of solitude and lonesomeness in the container.

I eventually made friends with an amazing French woman who made me pies and took care of my mental needs in trade for welding lessons. Her name is Anouchka Oler, and she introduced me to everyone as the boy who lives in a box in the harbor. At first, this was painful. I didn't like the idea that I was homeless. It was less of an adventure than most people seemed to think, and in fact, during this time, I started to think about what a home needs for it to be called, or even felt as a home. The box to me, was no home outside of its ability to provide shelter, and I soon came to realize that the things outside of a structure contribute just as much to homeness as what is inside.

> *Upon my return, this discussion became even more prevalent with my then roommate Ryan Hageman. We had both arrived back to Minneapolis from different trips abroad, and had experienced very different ways of living. Both of which seemed to*

induce an even greater sense of efficiency into our lives.
Ryan became an inspiration to my thoughts as he
counted the number of things he owned, and reduced
this number by selling his items in his Needless *sale.*
We came up with the term homeness-less to describe
the ability to maximize your homeness with less. And
while I may profess to these things, Ryan is a much
better example at living to these standards.

Anouchka lived with a few other people that I would get to know as well, one of whom was a great architecture enthusiast. As I was learning more and more about my own spatial needs, I started recognizing larger spaces, how they were useful, how they directed people, and how shapes and color can affect one's perceptions of space. The most obvious example of this came during the World Cup Finale between The Netherlands and Spain. I found my way to a street that could be heard from the harbor, and discovered a crowd of over 10,000 people covered in orange. Orange flags, orange jerseys, wigs, makeup, cars, horns, and even orange tulips falling from the sky! The landscape was surreal. As the match went on, orange fires burst into orange trash bins, and orange men shook the orange fence that I had climbed to watch the projection screen hundreds of feet away. In the last minutes of the game, you could sense the happiness turn into panic as The Netherlands was attempting to make a score. Shots on goal, but nothing. There was a tension within the crowd up front, but back where I was standing, drummers and fire starters had been consumed by their daze. Louder and louder the crowd grew, and then police in riot gear appeared. They must have been there the whole time, but their presence was only known to me now. The clock wound down and Spain won. The fantastic turned mundane in an instant. Everything stopped. There was no more sense of riot. The sound turned off. The fires died out. People walked home. It was one of the saddest things to watch as I slowly rode my bike back to the harbor. No one was talking, and the non-stop cheering seemed like it had never happened. It was back to the work week.

I was amazed at how this had all worked out. Like some sort of beautiful construction and deconstruction gone perfectly to plan. Nothing went out of line, and yet, it seemed as though it could have burst at the seams. Layer upon layer of orange had built a skyscraper that lay on its side in the street, and when the whistle blew, brick by brick it was removed and carefully set aside in its individual home, revealing the street on which it had rested. Scale and human force shed their light on this day.

> *While this story doesn't have much to do with the buildings I encountered in The Netherlands, and post-war Rotterdam, I assure you that these structures were there, in all of their majestic signature style. Instead, what makes me so interested, and maybe so against becoming an architect, are these moments that make me think of the surrounding space. Of events that trigger the ideas of size and instability. Of something unable to control. In most cases, these sensations are accompanied by buildings. I tend to relate this feeling of standing under a skyscraper, to that of swimming next to a whale in the ocean. Whales are my greatest fear, and also, one of my*

deepest desires. At any moment, this creature could swallow you whole, or fall into you and crush your very being. I think buildings have this same nature imbued into them, despite the engineers' taming efforts. But we trust our surroundings to professional builders, and we move on without question.

I have recently read the work of Franco La Cecla entitled "Against Architecture," and I am fortunate to have found someone who I agree with in many ways regarding the current practice of architecture. While I may not be one now, or ever, as pointed out in his book, I fantasize of the medium's ideologies, and am impressed with scale in most cases, whether it be a building, a marathon of runners, or a sea of glowing plankton beneath the boat. The human ability to construct and raise monuments that push physical boundaries is awe-inspiring, as well as distracting from the more-than-human world. As Abram puts it, "The super straight lines and right angles of our office architecture ... make our animal senses wither even as they support the abstract intellect; the wild, earth-born nature of the materials—the woods, clays, metals, and stones that went into the building—are readily forgotten behind the abstract and calculable form." As a builder myself, I search for the deeper relationship that is innate in creation. To know how materials work and react, is to better understand how to survive alongside them.

While covering Maurice Merleau-Ponty and the participatory nature of perception, Abram speaks to the reciprocal nature of touch and sight. "To touch the coarse skin of a tree is thus, at the same time, to experience one's own tactility, to feel oneself touched *by* the tree. And to see the world, is also, at the same time, to experience oneself as visible, to feel oneself *seen*."

After graduating from the art school I went to, I was accepted into a three-month teaching residency in Beijing, along with another school peer, and a third, who had graduated from elsewhere. My peer and myself were both white skinned, while our new companion was of Chinese decent. We had been accepted to help create cross-cultural curriculum and values within an up and coming group of art schools for kids.

I am fortunate to have seen so many different things during these past adventures, but it wasn't until this trip to Beijing, where I felt this reciprocity of "feeling oneself seen." In turn, I started to become more aware of how minorities can feel, specifically tied to issues of immigration, homosexuality and transgender. For those who have traveled to a country, or even moved into a new neighborhood where the majority of the human landscape's color, or values, are different than your own, this sensation is easy to recognize.

While it is customary to stare in Chinese culture, this feeling of being visible and my own seeing of the culture was not wholly amplified by these cultural habits alone. Being surrounded by a crowded sea of Chinese people (and all of its many ethnic minorities), seeing ads on TV for makeup that made you more "white," being a selling point for a business that capitalized on its "white" teachers, and enticed by the Chinese guests at Tiananmen Square to take pictures with them, despite being complete strangers, made me more vulnerable to my own presence, and more specifically, the visibleness that others can feel.

Having come from a place where I had taken these differences for granted, I quickly recognized my self. I was reacquainted with the importance of color and its attachment to human skin, history, politics, and social constructs. Maybe even more basic, its connections to the sensations of touch, smell, taste, and sound. My whiteness felt intrusive, or intimidating as I walked onto the subways and into restaurants. While at the same time, the over-valued white teacher was awkward in comparison to the Chinese teacher who worked many times harder, yet received little praise. While it may seem like this was simply a kind gesture from the school's directors, there was a definite difference in treatment for our cohort of Chinese decent. The expectations for her were much different. She garnered little praise it seemed in comparison to the two of us, and yet also worked twice as hard, translating and serving as a sort of intermediary. It was uncomfortable. Even in day-to-day life, vendors and strangers assumed she must know the language, but didn't. I soon began to think about the various demographics in Minneapolis, and the discomfort that they can encounter. My thoughts went first to the Somalis, Hispanics, and the queer community.

My awkward feelings of difference were not "hardships," but it led me to begin thinking about the possible and innate struggles that Others have had to endure. While Merleau-Ponty suggests that we feel ourself touched by the tree, he doesn't suggest that we can *be* the tree touching ourselves, only that we know touch through the being touched by of others, and our previous knowledge of how touch feels. In fact, it would be wrong to become the tree, for if we were all trees, who would jump into our leaves, or climb our branches to see new heights? We need each other, and I feel that it is important to learn from each other, but it is quite foolish to try and become each other. A path towards empathy became something I wanted, and knowing full well the impossibleness of complete empathy, it became just that, a path *towards* empathy.

So maybe this is where my personal introduction to the inquiry began to correspond with my subjective objective. To continue learning from others, including what we may perceive to be non-human. To become a participant on the path towards empathy. To bring an awareness to the fact that we can't help everyone, but that we can open and train our minds to change our perceptions and mental attitudes, and that *can* help everyone. To know that it is important to take care of yourself before taking care of others, in an understanding that you can't truly take care of yourself without letting others help you and vice versa. To face discomfort, in order to have a better relationship with comfort. To keep your senses open, and to participate, in order to shed the line that separates "us" from connecting with "them." And in Abram's words, "to give voice to the world from our experienced situation *within* it, recalling us to our participation in the here-and-now, rejuvenating our sense of wonder at the fathomless things, events and powers that surround us on every hand."

Care is one of those things you can lose sight of every once in a while, especially in times of discomfort. This story is about Michael, who became one of the biggest helpers in picking me up from a post-graduation funk, and through this memory of him, continues to be an inspiration to me.

Michael was a second grader at the time. He is the younger brother of another boy, who I never fully met, but in many ways, I could empathize with Michael in the sense that I am also the younger brother in my family. I only saw the two of them interact while they waited for the bus, but it was easy to see the familiarity. He looked up to his brother just as much as I did mine. He was chubbier, weaker, and just a tad shorter than his brother, soon to outgrow him. He wanted to hang with the older boys just as I did, and when he was rejected by them, he moved on to play with his own peers, all of which happened to be girls, just like my own experiences when I was younger. For myself, there was rarely ever a boy my age in the after school programs, summer camps, or Sunday school classrooms. Michael was sensitive and caring. In fact, there were many moments when Michael showed me how to care, but it was one particular act of kindness that helped me understand how important caring really is.

I met Michael because I was the Introduction to Graphic Design teacher for a small after-school program that hosted students from a 95% free and reduced lunch school. This means that most of the families are considered to be living in high poverty. Since the students were coming to this after school program, it usually meant also that their parents worked multiple jobs in order to sustain the costs of having a family, and were unable to pick their children up after school. The students were aware of all of this, as it was blatantly talked about around them, but Michael was unfazed. He always carried a smile with him. Maybe he was choosing to ignore these factors, maybe he was unaware, or maybe he was just truly happy with where he was whenever I saw him.

The idea of an introduction to graphic design course seemed silly for an after-school program that had a room full of broken down computers with Microsoft Word and limited access internet. I wasn't exactly sure what to do, especially as I had dropped out of design myself, and moved onto sculpture during my studies at college. We started with an introduction of each other, and what we thought design was. No one quite knew, nor did anyone care, and since my classes are geared towards my students, we renamed the class to Super Happy Awesome Fun Time, or SHAFT, which, in it's acronym form, was always kept secret and only served as my little "flipping of the finger" to a system that I felt was seriously shafting these students. We started with a poster project. The students spread out onto the floor and I went through a list of questions. Each student would write their answers, and by the end of this long list of inquiries, their pieces of paper would be filled with words, and be a sort of portrait of their lives. What is your favorite color? Who do you care about the most? What is your favorite food? Where would you like to travel? Who is your best friend? What do you want to be when you grow up? Easy questions, mixed with others that might be less common in the lives that these students led.

We moved onto the computer room in future lessons and flipped the monitors on their sides to use as light tables to trace their favorite things. We made birthday cards for some of my friends, and even get well cards for a sick dog named Brogan that I fell in love with in Ohio. There eventually came a time when I had to resort to my backup lesson plan which was a simple internet scavenger hunt. "Who was the 16th president?" "Who is the 44th president?" "Who is Dilma Rousseff?" Learning how to find answers to clues like these using a basic search engine was the skill to be learned in these lessons. It became a competition, and students raced to find the answers. The prize was a king-size chocolate bar. Michael was one of the faster students at finding these answers, and had a pretty good chance of winning, that is, if he had decided to stay on course.

Internet scavenger hunts are seemingly easy. Read the clue, type in the clue to your search engine, find the answer. But imagine that all of the clues are suddenly in a foreign language, one that uses characters you've never even seen before. One of my students was unable to speak or read English at all, and so you can imagine the frustration that this list of clues must have brought him. During our previous lessons, students were more or less free to do what they wanted within the lesson's themes. So it wasn't until now that I became aware of this language barrier. This time, there was more direction, and even less context to be looking around to try and understand what one should be doing. This boy, whose name was Eh-koo-too, was sitting next to Michael, and you could tell he was starting to panic.

Enter Michael, the second-grade-saint. As I turned back around from helping another student to see if Eh-koo-too was faring any better, I saw something truly amazing. Michael had stopped working on his scavenger hunt and turned his chair to be closer to Eh-koo-too. Michael sat there next to the keyboard and showed each letter to Eh-koo-too, sounding each one out as he pointed to it on the paper, and then showed where it was on the keyboard, and how when you pressed the key down, it also appeared on the screen. "This is how you do it," he said. Michael did several of the clues for Eh-koo-too and then moved on to letting Eh-koo-too try the keyboard. As if he was now the older brother, Michael was teaching Eh-koo-too how to recognize letters, and words, and the meanings of words as their picture counterparts appeared on the screen as they were typed. He continued to do this for the rest of the class.

The next best thing happened when Michael's mom came and knocked on the door, exclaiming that they were leaving early to go out for Michael's birthday dinner. Wait a second. WHAT?! You're telling me that it's his birthday and he's still doing these amazing things? Michael was truly selfless. He showed a level of care on a day that should have been dedicated to himself. His actions were unprecedented for a second-grader. He quickly packed his bag and left the class while Eh-koo-too continued working by himself. There was no concern for the candy bar prize. I was in a bit of shock as class continued as usual.

In weeks following, it was great to see Michael hanging out with Eh-koo-too before and after class, and even sticking up for him at times. I was so amazed that someone could rise above all of the factors trying to hold him back, only to find himself reach back down into the mess of it all, and pick another person up to join him. At the end of the semester, I was able to share this story at family day where the whole community came together for a big dinner. I'm so proud to have had him as a student, and so fortunate to have had him as my teacher. It's important to take care of yourself and find a clearing in the fog, but once there, finding Others to share it with becomes even more important. And to understand that when we unknowingly drift outside of the clear, we must attain an openness so that Others can help bring us back too.

There is currently a man in the rainforest of Papua New Guinea. He belongs to the Sawiyano Tribe, and he is their hunter. He ventures out each night to bring back food for the village, and if the hunt is unsuccessful, he gathers from his garden to spread amongst his community. He provides food to those who are too old, or too sick to work themselves. He is strong, but gentle; intimidating, yet open. Though he is not the leader, he takes care of the tribe he belongs to. His name is Raphael Mera, and he is my latest role model and inspiration.

Raphael must have met me before I ever really met him, as the news of two white visitors had become a big story in the jungle. I imagine him having eyed Bethany and me as we got out of the little Cessna plane that delivered us to the grassy airstrip located two hours from their village. While we were met with flower necklaces and crushed orchid petals to our foreheads, Raphael was taking care of more important things, like helping his son, keeping care of an elder, or falling into line with the other villagers who unpacked the plane and carried our supplies to their home. He did not worry himself with the excitement of our arrival. I think I remember him hugging Bethany, as she had grown up in the village and was more or less family, but I on the other hand, was a stranger, and not yet familiar with the scene. We might have shaken hands, but I like to think that we didn't meet each other because of his own humbleness and protective eye. The more lively introduction happened later that night when we brought out the soccer balls.

Like the strongest first grader on the playground, Raphael burst into the small area we had marked off between the raised huts, and kicked the ball as hard as he could! It went flying into the bush as he smiled and hollered loudly. Everyone laughed and applauded his great kick. After one of the younger boys brought back the ball, we started again and Raphael did the same thing. SMASH! The ball went flying, nearly missing a baby's head. He smiled and hollered and everyone laughed again. I started to become annoyed, because this kept happening with even greater recklessness until finally, I started playing against him. I dribbled the ball slowly, quickly maneuvering around his strong, but clumsy, soccer feet. Every time he approached me to kick the ball I would slide it from under him, causing his foot to completely miss the ball and make him trip or fall. Everyone including Raphael laughed and hollered. He was persistent and wouldn't give up, always excited to get back and try again until he succeeded. Though maybe he too was getting frustrated, having to learn how the soccer ball and feet could work together to create traps, a strategy which I learned he used for hunting. I knew he was paying attention because when he finally got the ball back he approached me slowly with it, teasing me to come forward. As I approached, he brought back his foot for another huge kick and just as everyone covered, or turned away, and before he made contact, he stopped his foot and completely faked us out, tapping the ball to my other side, losing control of it, tripping onto the ground face first, and failing to coordinate his trick. Though a valiant effort, everyone fell over laughing, including Raphael and myself. From then on, he became one of my greatest friends in the tribe.

He took me on walks to various places around the village. He took me to the tallest tree we could find. He educated me on various plants, insects, and other wildlife. We gathered coconuts from their old village site. We hollered and made songs throughout our walks. He spent several weeks tracking and catching a wild boar because we had mentioned wanting to taste one. He dropped off pumpkins to our hut each night without asking for anything in return. He brought me to the site where his father was buried, and what I knew was a taboo subject to talk about, he discussed him with me, specifically his love and hate for him. We cried together, continuing this discussion towards his role as a widower father, and his felt responsibility for his son and daughter, despite tribal norms. And it is this opening up of concern and care that makes me regard him so highly.

Raphael is the epitome of what you might call a progressive tribesman. He is the brother of the leader of the tribe, and thus, highly regarded and well-liked within the culture. Though he isn't the leader, he does what he thinks is necessary in taking care of the tribe, and not simply himself. With this direct relation, as well as being a male and the village hunter, he navigates the social norms with great leniency. For example, a few months before we arrived, Raphael's wife had passed away. From what other villagers said, it had been especially hard on him. Unlike other arranged marriages, they were very much in love. In order to escape taboo, Raphael moved out of the hut where they had lived, and moved in with his brother. Though, unlike the cultural norms, he refused to accept a lower status and responsibility. He gave his daughter to his mother for caring, but refused to give up his son. He also refused to accept a new wife in order to take over the female tasks that exist in their typical family structure. Instead, Raphael did everything he did before, in addition to what his wife had been doing. He continued to hunt, gather from his garden, and provide for the village. He also gathered firewood, bathed his son, cooked meals, washed the clothes, and made conversation. Though still respectful of his mourning period, he wanted to maintain his role within the village, and not fall for the cultural norm "traps" of their society.

It was easy to see how good of a person Raphael was. He wasn't selfish. He was strict. He had clear definitions of right and wrong, but also understood compassion and the appropriate times to allow for those definitions to change. He lived simply. He wasn't fazed by technology introduced to the tribe. His brother, as well as the rest of the tribe, had accumulated many things from missionaries over the years, yet, Raphael had left these nonessential objects alone. Though, he did accept several gifts from Bethany and I for hunting: a knife, waterproof bag, water bottle, and solar flashlight. He also accepted a few bars of soap to bathe his son with. He understands the difference between useful and useless.

Several days before our departure, Raphael insisted on taking me back to the old site of their village where they still gathered coconuts from. It would be one last walk through the jungle, one last gathering of coconuts, and one last time to be together. As usual, Raphael led the walk, hooting and hollering, cutting down trees that I might hit my head on, and announcing fragile pathways. And like every trip before, several younger boys and his son had decided to join along. We had walked this path several times before, and it still hadn't changed.

As we arrived at the site, we gathered broken coconut shells and fashioned seats from them. After surveying which trees were promising of good coconuts, Raphael began right away to scale them, machete in his mouth. Once reaching the top, he yelled for the boys to get out of the way while he chopped down the drupes, letting them fall from their great height. They made a great whooshing noise as they zoomed to the ground and plopped onto the soft earth. After a dozen or so coconuts had been cut, he yelled for the boys to gather them, and hurried back down to help.

We gathered the fallen coconuts and brought them back to a circle where we sat. Raphael and one of the boys, Lemax, began shedding the layers of our snacks with their machetes, handing them first to me, and then fixing one for themselves. After drinking every last bit of our opened coconuts, we split them open, using the shells to scoop out the meat. Raphael and the boys kept hollering, stuffing their faces with coconut, and laughing over memorable moments we all had together. After eating, we all had to answer nature's call and empty our bladders. I walked away from the group and found what seemed like a carved out hole. I unzipped but was hesitant. Soon, Raphael was right behind me and we both stared down at the hole. I zipped back up and Raphael revealed that this was where his father was buried. My first thought was how glad I was that I hadn't peed in that hole. My second thought was to continue the conversation, asking when he had passed, and how his relationship with his father was. Raphael didn't hesitate to say how good of a father he was, that he learned a lot from him, and that he cared very much for his father. He paused though after saying this, and began to say, but he was a very hard father to have. He was very violent. He beat my mother. He beat other men in the tribe. It was a different time, and he wasn't the only violent man. Raphael loved his father, yet there were so many aspects of him that he seemed disappointed with. When I asked him, Raphael admitted that this was why he thought the tribe was currently at peace. That they had seen so much violence growing up, they refused to carry it into the future. They wanted to be happy, and they would not tolerate this behavior of the past. In fact, there was a woman who was seen beating her son one day, and members of the tribe rushed over to stop her, yelling at her and shaming her as a mother. Raphael did not reveal any specifics of his own encounters with violence from his father, but he made it clear that this was what caused their love hate relationship, and I began to reflect on parallel experiences.

The notion of having something so deeply affect you that it changes the way you approach the future is interesting. I think that this is a very basic lesson that is reinforced through traveling, studying history, and reflecting upon one's past. It is good to learn from our own mistakes at times, and may be the only way to retain the power of their consequences, but we cannot forget that many mistakes have already been made for us. We shouldn't ignore history to the point where we begin to repeat its disasters. Easier said than done, we can begin simply by being more open to Others, more aware of the choices we make, take more care to make more effort, and move in a direction towards empathy and understanding of our interconnected life world.

I am so very grateful to have met Raphael during my trip to Papua New Guinea. The level of care and effort that he made for his son, as well as the community he lived in, despite cultural norms, was astounding. He taught through his actions and inspired by example. Rarely explicit, his spirit encouraged smiling, laughing, fun and happiness. He is a full foot shorter than I am, and when we hugged before my departure, we held each other and cried. With our heads together, his feet dangled in the air, and as if for the first time, he was the one being supported, his hardened feet unearthed and able to breathe in new life-air for the both of us.

The Sawiyano tribe taught me Tok Pisin and other lessons in the form of drawings and short stories. We practiced drawing and writing together. Below is a translation of Benjamin's stories.

Benjamin Mera

This is a story about animals (prey) and the garamut (drum).

1. There is a bird that flies very high. And this bird sits in tree.

2. But the tree kangaroo only walks along the ground. He just eats the little trees.

3. The bandicoot, he also finds food on the ground.

4. The garamut's (slit-gong drum) work is this: to tell us of sad times, of news, and when it's time for church.

I think that is all, my story about the garamut. Thank you for listening. That is it, goodbye. For you, Brian

BENjamin MERA RaS boy
Wapalu VILLAGE

Em Stori pilong apus na Karama

1 pisin Em Save frai antap tru.
Na em Save sinlaun Long diwai,
Tasol

2 Sikau em man pilong Wokapaut
Long ~~gra~~ girann tasol.
Em Save Kaikai pilsinini diWai tasol

3 mamut Em tu Save painim kaikai,
Long grau tasol

4 Wok pilong karamt em olsem
~~Hevi~~ Hevi taim Na sumbela,
Tok tok Na Lotu.
Ating em tasol Stori bilong karant
thankiyu Long hari bilong yu.
Em tasol gut bai,
Long yu Brain

#new toe

1992. Pirate brothers at Horn Creek Ranch. *Photo by Karen Huffman.*

2010. Overlooking Killary Fjord in Ireland with Kinji Akagawa and Maxwell Grove. *Photo by Megan Drmota.*

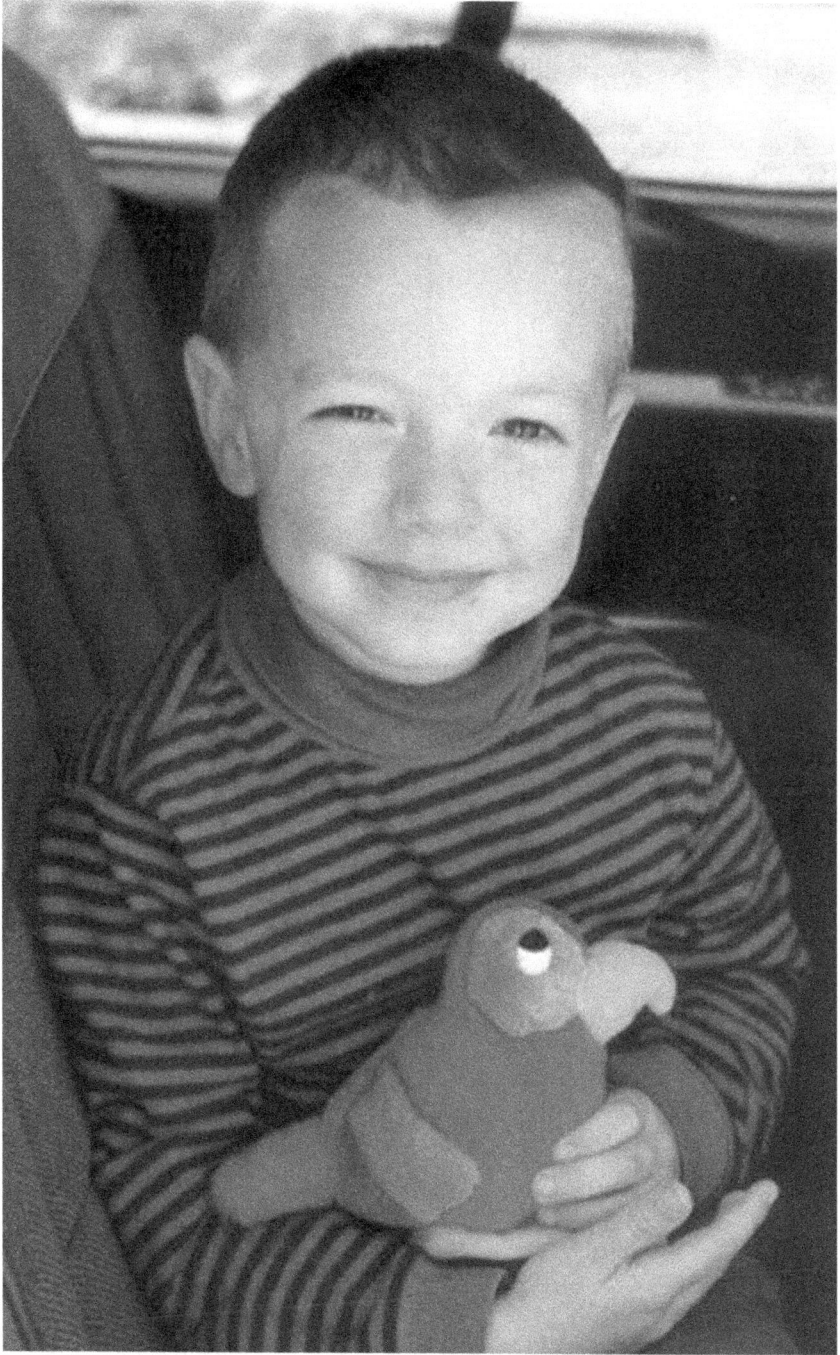

1992. Inside the family van with my souvenir parrot. *Photo by Karen Huffman.*

2012. Celebrating a successful day of fishing with the Sawiyano bois.

2012. Filimon, of the Sawiyano Tribe, had gotten a horrible cough. We had him go underneath a blanket and breathe in steam from medicinal plants. Bethany and I joked about Joseph Beuys.

2012. Raphael Mera, and his son, Nantex.

2010. The Rotterdam crowd at the World Cup finale between The Netherlands and Spain.

2010. Overlooking Rotterdam with Anouchka Oler.

2011. Playing in Beijing with one of the school girls. *Photo by Ming Ming.*

2011. Painting on Canvas, a performance collaboration with my friend Alex in Beijing. She had majored in "Traditional Painting on Canvas." *Photo by Ming Ming.*

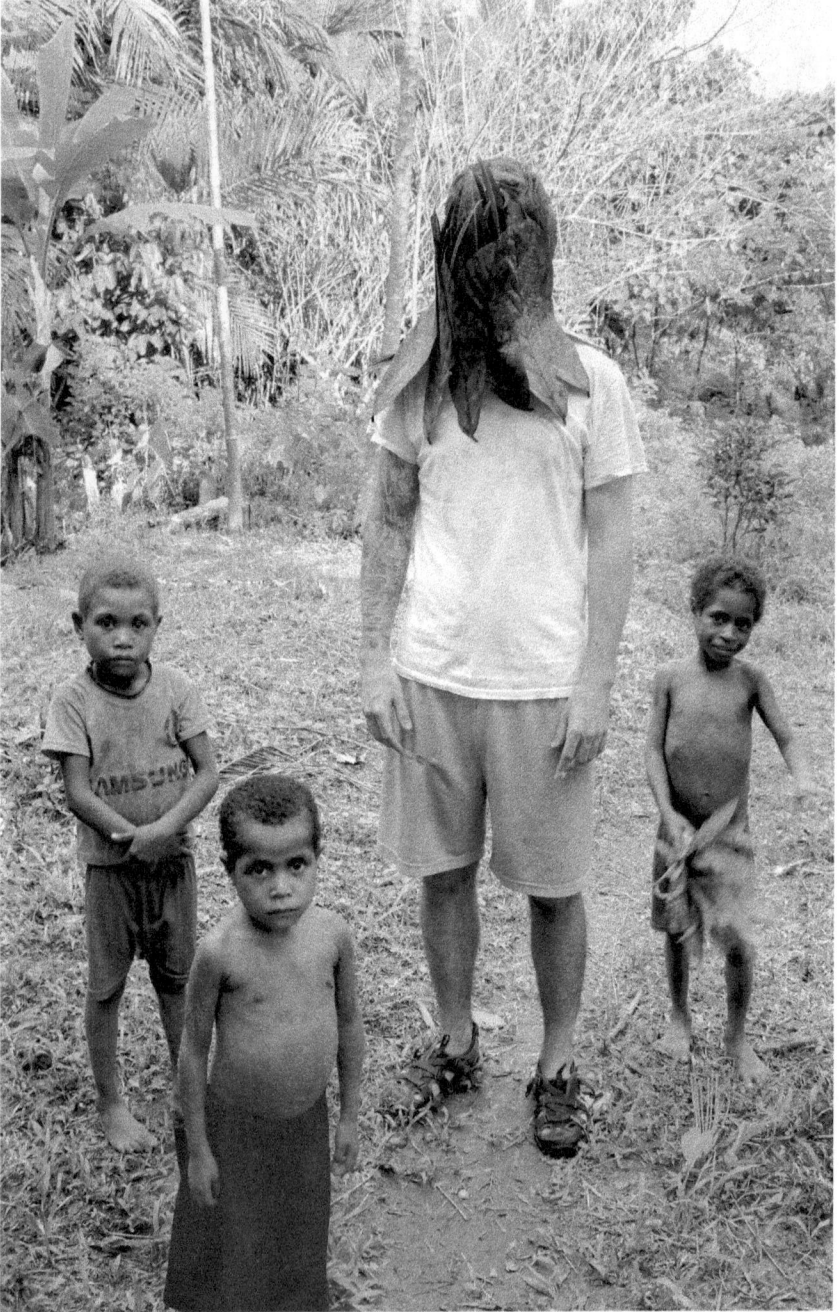

2012. Playing with some Sawiyano kids in my Jungle Head mask. *Photo by Bethany Kalk.*

2012. Eating coconuts at the old-home site with Raphael, Nantex, Lemax, Ishmael, and another village boi.

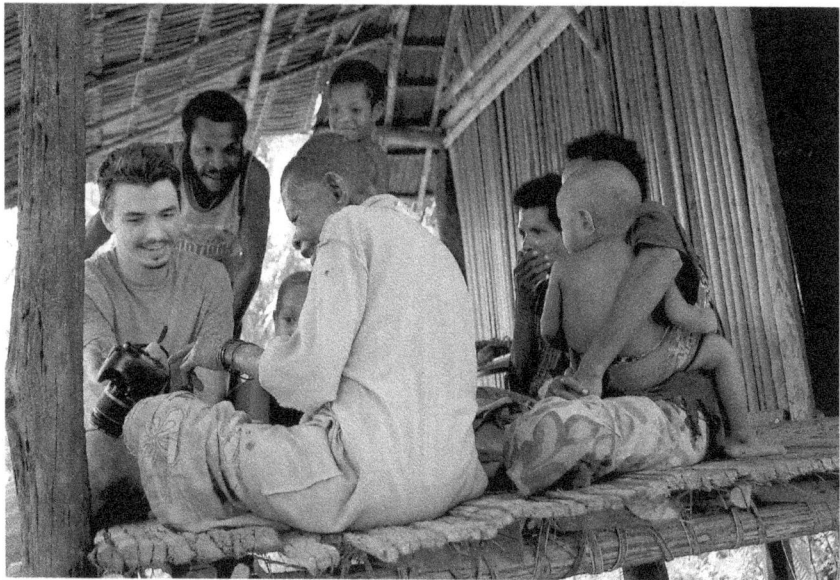

2012. One of the elders sees a photograph of herself for the first time. *Photo by Bethany Kalk.*

2012. Borem learns how to use a camera, while James waves in the background.

2012. Sitting on a fallen tree branch, sharing photos with Lemax and a village boi.
Photo by Bethany Kalk.

2012. Bob Mera, the leader of the Sawiyano Tribe, returns home with a wild boar for dinner.

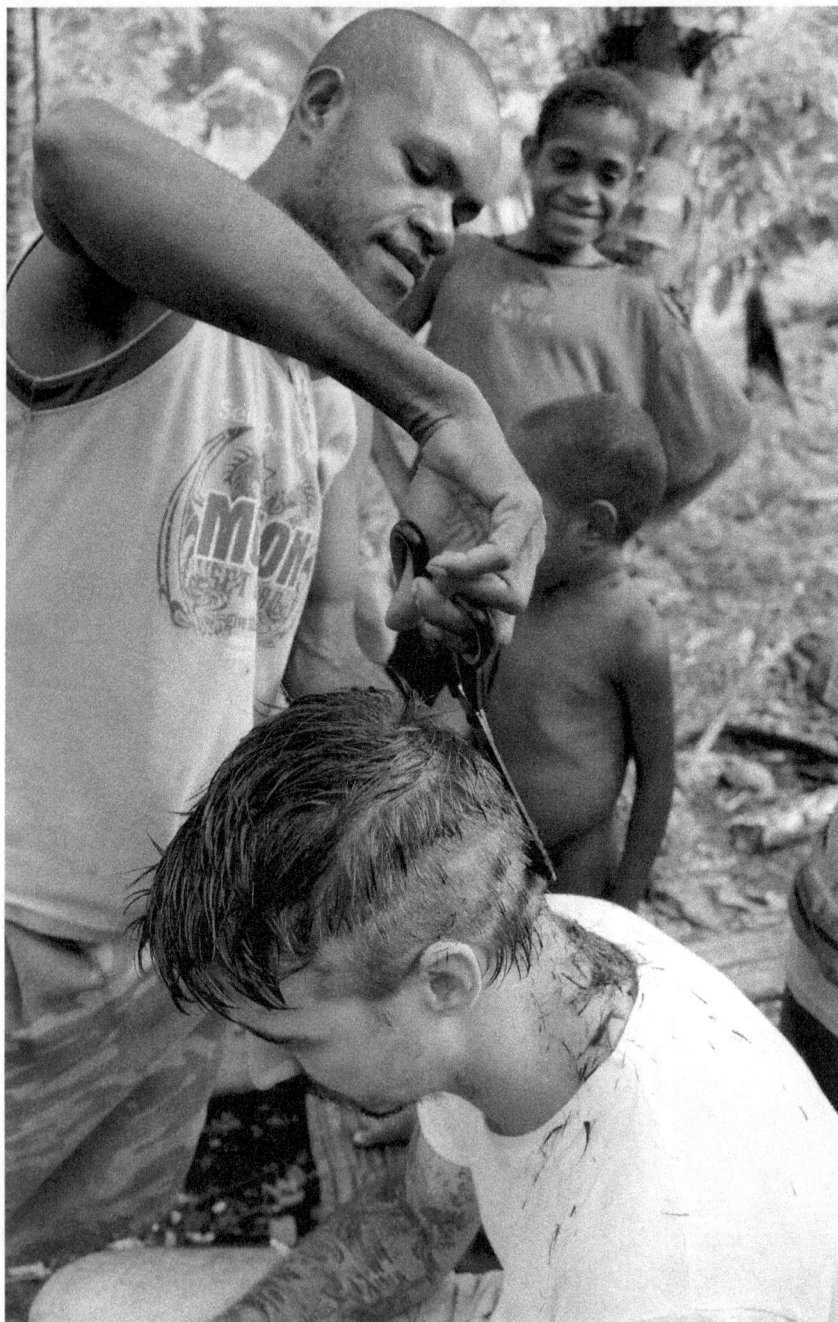

2012. Benjamin, of the Sawiyano Tribe, cuts a white person's hair for the first time. It is the best haircut I have ever received. *Photo by Bethany Kalk.*

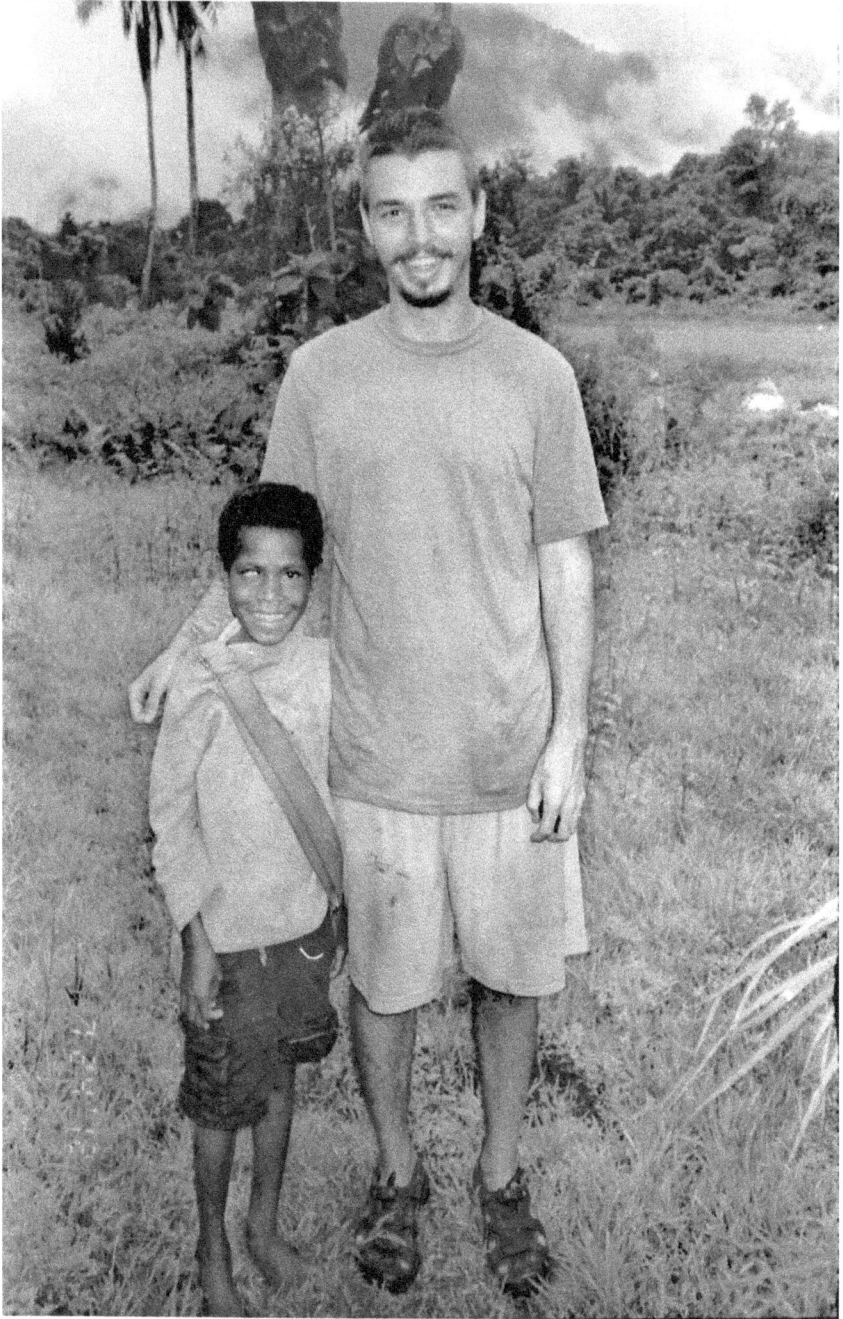

2012. Me and LeMax, my constant companion throughout PNG. *Photo by Bethany Kalk.*

2012. Denny, of the Sawiyano Tribe, gives me a tattoo using battery acid, water, and a sewing needle. We share the same mark. *Photo by Bethany Kalk.*

2010. Dancing in the streets of Rotterdam under the guise of my Visible Man outfit. *Photo by Anouchka Oler.*

2011. Little Tiger holds up his painting in the toddler art class in Beijing.

2011. The opening of *Pop Saw The Need*, a one-night opening at the Double Art Gallery in Minneapolis, Minnesota, with Jenny Bookler, Maxwell Grove, Kinji Akagawa, Maura Kelly Doyle, Alyson Coward, Kelly Filreis, and Nick Jackson. *Photo by Pat Bookler.*

Gro bye Abraham Tony

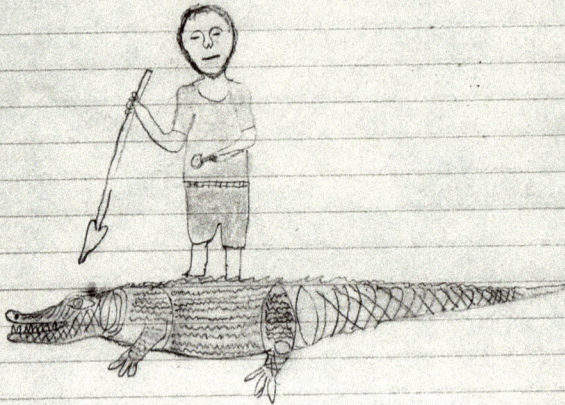

Olol PukPuk i slip i stap.
Papa i laik kilim wanpela PukPuk
Papa i apim spia tasol PukPuk i
opim ai na i laik paitim papa.
Papa i lap long PukPuk i laik
pait long em. Spia pilong papa i
kisim PukPuk. Pinis.
naip pilong Papa i katim PukPuk.
ol i amamas long Papa i kilim
PukPuk. em tasol liklik stoli
pilong em

Gro bye

Abraham's Story

The crocodile is there sleeping.

Papa wants to kill a crocodile.

Papa raised his spear but the crocodile opened his eye and wanted to fight with Papa.

Papa laughed because the crocodile wanted to fight with him.

Papa's spear killed the crocodile.

Papa's knife cut up the crocodile.

Everyone celebrated that Papa had killed the crocodile.

That is all, his little story.

CONVERSATIONS

This section contains thoughts from conversations I've had with friends. They range in topic from patterns found at home, where we are, what we think is happening, what we think we can do, and how we think we should be.

I constantly return to the idea of care, hoping to figure out what it is, and how best it can be used. For the most part, I think that for different people, there come to be different kinds of care, and that they must all exist for this idea of caring to remain at all. But what I like to think about is how we disperse of our care. How we come to care, how we decide to implement it, and how, in times of hardship, our care can become stretched thin, creating a perception of non-care onto ourselves and Others.

While I'm not at all into a quantification of such qualitative things, I usually like to create basic equations for how I see things. Caring is a very simple accumulation of sums, but depending on how you prioritize and take care of these sums, it can become very difficult to manage.

Let's say that everyone has a maximum of 100 care points, and that there are different sections of caring. We'll start off simple by looking at our day-to-day responsibilities. Removing any kind of interest/hobby variables, I like to start with the number of jobs one has. 25 points of care can be given to each job. With only 100 points, this may seem like a lot, especially if you work multiple jobs. It easily adds up when you account for the care points dedicated to things like cleanliness, future aspirations, eating and family. If you've had four jobs like me, you may have failed to care about anything else, 4 x 25 = 100 = nothing left to care about. Although, if you have other things in life that require care, i.e., a child, you may need to dedicate a large number of care points to them. Let's say that only one of those jobs is really worth all 25 points. We can take away 15 points from the other three, allowing 45 points of care for your child. You'll continue to make the same amount of money as you did before, you'll just care less about three of those other jobs. That comes to 25 + (10 x 3) + 45 = 100 = stressful, but doable. Throw in some future aspirations, emotional drama, and student loans, and you're equation can start to get messier and messier.

But there's a bigger catch. Your caring is directly related to how others care. How you care for yourself, affects not only how people care for themselves, but how they care for you too. We don't just care for physical things or beings, we also care about how we feel, and how Others feel around us. But when our caring points are spread so thin, it's hard to dedicate enough care to make it seem like we do. Once our priorities and dedication of points is easily recognizable, it's even easier for Others to tell what you really care about, and thus, not care as much about. Some are better at hiding this, but it usually takes a toll on the caring they dedicate to themselves, and all the meanwhile, people who dedicate time to caring about how much Others don't care, are losing care points dedicated to themselves.

This is why it's important to take care of yourself before you take care of Others. Others are people, animals, plants, mountains, forests, etc. It is impossible to help Others past the point of you having helped yourself. We must start with ourselves, where we gain our primal perspectives from. Our selves are the basis for what we compare all Other things to. It is at once easy to see through someone who cares very little for you, and maybe in this day and age, it can seem a bit grim. As one continues on the path to take care of the self, it must be understood that this care can only be achieved when Others are allowed to take care of you and vice versa; a true interdependence starting to emerge.

After coming back from Beijing, I worked as an after school teacher, twice a week, working with students aged 7 to 12. I was asked to be the introduction to graphic design teacher for a program that provided me 14 computers with Microsoft Word and limited access internet. The class itself was a challenge, but doable and exciting with many ways to experiment. The other teachers involved were unable to care about the program. It was an hour out of each day for these teachers, and being just one of their four jobs, it was understandable. Maybe this multiplicity of jobs is a normal aspect of life I just haven't realized yet, but it was very obvious that these teachers dedicated very little care to this job. I myself had several other jobs; gardener, gallery assistant and pizza delivery driver; all jobs that in the end, didn't seem to have as much social value as working with my students, and thus, had a cap of very minimal care points. The biggest problem here is that the students could see straight through the teachers, and thus, didn't care too much for them either. This created a cycle of not-caring that snowballed into chaotic classrooms and hyperactivity.

For the teachers, it was an hour out of each day, a transition to the next job, and something that they simply needed to "get past." It only became this way because of bigger economic issues that forced a lack of care points into the situation. Even though the teachers might have wanted to care, there simply weren't enough care points to go around.

It must be an ideology of ours then, that we end up with one job that creates for us, a comfortable situation, that will allow us to spend freely the rest of our care points how we please. Only a few fall into this scenario, because more and more, I meet people with multiple jobs. They say they would like to have one job that can pay all the bills, save some money, have constant hours, and is "fun." This is rare, especially as American society speeds up, forcing people to try and grasp their future at younger ages, not ever fully knowing their interests.

When I was in high-school, we were expected to be thinking about which colleges we would be going to as sophomores, and I still regret how fast it went. I started thinking that, like my brother, I would go to the United States Naval Academy. Unfortunately, I hated the idea of marching and being yelled at as it brought me straight back to my childhood. I came back from the Academy's summer seminar, dropped out of my advanced math and science classes, and went back to art, something I had left behind freshman year as careers started being talked about. I wasn't quite sure what would happen with art, but I felt compelled. I went straight from high school to an art college, and during those four years of college, I felt like I had done everything right, aside from skipping out on a few gallery openings. I graduated on time, and like so many other Americans, I was out of school at 22.

While age doesn't exactly account for experience, it seems to be a common conception that youth is not an asset for leadership positions, and should be doubted (unless of course, youth accompanies a smaller pay rate). I say this because I had several interviews for program coordinator positions after Beijing that I was extremely excited about. Each of these interviews ended in a similar fashion. "We really love your ideas and what you want to do, but we just can't trust a program to a 22 year-old." I suppose it makes sense. Other staff members might feel awkward working "underneath" someone younger than them, but I grew increasingly frustrated. I graduated from what I thought was a top-of-the-line school that everyone would respect, to go on a journey to set up art schools in Beijing, and then to come back to rejection after rejection for being too young. I had the energy to move things and get things done. I hadn't yet been tainted by the evils of bureaucracy and formalities. I was a ball of energy with huge ideas, and it started me thinking about how our system might be failing (in relation to complacency, comfort, and attitudes against risk), and how slowing down may help, or not help, and why in the end, it has been a great fortune to not have received these positions. Easily summed up, the discomfort in these instances only added fuel to the fire, allowing me to find comfort in a continued passion for my future aspirations and travel.

In fact, in Europe I found out that most of the people I met had taken off a year or two after high-school to travel. To travel! Such a simple thing like this is unheard of in the States. Travel incited a new sense of self for my friends abroad and a new independent confidence and ambition. While in the states, we harness ambition and confidence from test scores and teachers telling us we'll go far in this subject or that subject. Though we never know, or find out for ourselves if we're really interested in these subjects, because we have not taken time off, away from them, to see if we truly long for them. We need to slow down in order to care more, at least in the initial stages to see where we should prioritize our care points. Otherwise, we will continue to be careless. Simply stated, it is of my understanding that we only have so many care points to place, so it is crucial to be careful when caring.

Before going to Papua New Guinea I started to have conversations about our roles and responsibilities with regards to Others. Specifically with respect towards indigenous tribal culture. I hoped to enter Papua New Guinea with these thoughts, and return with a better answer, or approach to the conversation. There are definite problems that face the tribes, but what exactly are we supposed to do? What can we do for the tribes of Papua New Guinea after we have become aware of them? Are they too far removed for us to care? Should it be *our* responsibility to do something about it? What good is there in discussing these issues? There will always be problems in this big earth, and they are problems that modern civilization has initiated. The tribes are entering into a social pattern of being "taken-over," kicked out and destroyed. With mining companies buying their land for less than minimal costs, and depleting it of all its resources. We are forced to remember what the native tribes of this land that we call America had to endure. Is there a responsibility to step in and protect the land and its people, or is it just one more thing we have to edit from our awareness? For aren't we aware of many problems that we cannot help?

If the land is preserved and left alone, and tribes are allowed to continue dwelling in these places away from modern civilization, maybe they will continue to live in their already assumed day-to-day lives, and exist in the traditional patterns. While the rest of earth goes on, these tribes will continue to live in this tiny closed-off society. With the lack of nourishment, and growth in diseases, the tribe will slowly waste away, from what might be perceived as natural causes, even though our interdependency has affected their culture with pollution, inappropriate technology, and western germs.

Ignoring the situation will bring a different result. Tribes who have been forced out of their land have had to move to the coasts, into other territories, or have simply died. No tribes are able to survive off of their land once it has been tainted with nickel-solutions and other kinds of distress. Very few members make it into modern civilization and are able to communicate well enough for work. The land itself is never able to rejuvenate, after having its thousand-year-old minerals stripped from its back.

I like to look back at what Abram said regarding our more-than-man-made societies. Living in Minneapolis, I feel pretty fortunate to be living in what is considered a "green city." When in reality, the green is in fact a pseudo-green. The trees have all been placed by man, the river has been built up with dams and the sky is streaked with steam from factories. Even what we consider to be natural has been taken over by man. Minnehaha Park is a beautiful place to be, and yet each viewpoint, each path, and each experience has been laid out by man, for man. We create systems to help superimpose this feeling of nature onto oneself, rather than trusting nature to do so by itself. This became apparent to me when I visited the

Needles in South Dakota and realized that the highways had been built and planned around specific outlook points. The adventure had been laid out, thus, extinguishing the adventure altogether. All I need to do is hop into my man-made car, drive onto this man-made highway, and see this man-made viewpoint. I might even say that my trips up north to the boundary waters have been tainted of man-madeness. For as I was looking for a new place to experience, I was suggested to certain locations within the boundary waters, and several specific spots to explore. While it seemed untouched, the previous man-made knowledge had made my experience seem less open to the natural world.

In regards to the tribes then, I see the destruction of land being one more way of taking out what is truly natural, and in doing so, harmful to our earth-friend. While our culture of immediacy is mostly run on money, there needs to be an immediate pause that happens when we start taking things away that cannot be given back. In Franco La Cecla's words, "The fear of the grotesque represented by cities today, their borders, their canyons and abysses that open up in the midst of known places, whether they be Parisian banlieues or stretches of sprawl. It's not by chance that a great part of the world is falling into desuetude, into indifference, into being unable to take on the burden of its own upkeep, of human caring. The primary effect of speed is distraction."

Upon my arrival, and after further reflection, yes, there are definitely many difficulties that face the tribe. Along with simply not having access to medicine, the tribes are also unaware of many good-health practices and face various health issues.

Some include the dietary needs of pregnant women and newborns, congestion caused by keeping fires inside of their homes without any ventilation, and the effects of smoking. Ways in which to amend these health issues can be taught, but are hard to maintain as the practices are tightly intertwined with their culture and tradition.

Even when medicine is available, tribes are not educated on its proper usage. In many cases, when the pain goes away, a tribe member will stop taking the prescription, forgoing the completion of doses, and causing the sickness to return. I presume that this is because they have not spent enough time with modern medicine to understand its rules. This approach echoes their traditional practices that provide short-term relief, such as rubbing a poisonous leaf on your forehead to remove a headache. Even though, after a short time, the headache returns and another leaf must be found. The government once supplied medicine and had an outpost nearby that could help, but not only was the government inconsistent with supplies, the tribes didn't know how to use the medicine correctly. With inconsistent government help, and a lack of awareness, the tribes continue to have great sicknesses within their village. During our visit, one woman died from tuberculosis. She had been sent to the hospital in town for treatment, but due to an early return home, she died several months later from not finishing her medicine.

Steam distilling alcohol has also sprung up in some villages and has caused terrible complications. As villagers become sick and vomit around their houses, flies and rodents are attracted. As the creatures grow in number, they then move onto the food that the tribe has gathered, ruining their food supply. This in turn causes the tribes to starve, and eventually can wipe out a whole group of people. They also speak of their minds becoming corrupt, as they become easily prone to violent hallucinations and attacking once the beverage has been consumed. Similar problems like this exist in our own country, and only reiterates the need to be responsible. Though health is a major issue, it is not a problem that is necessarily decimating the tribes. There are bigger problems that are factoring into their lives. Problems that may be out of our control.

Not all contact with the outside world has been beneficial for the tribes. In fact, I would argue that most of the contact, aside from some medical programs, has been detrimental. Many religious missionaries, which are the predominant contact for the tribes, have been conducting practices that lead the tribes down a road of dependency and remiss. While some people may see conversion as a problem (as do I), it seems less of a problem to me, than the actual ways in which the missionaries conduct their relationship with the tribes. With the presence of missionaries, also comes the presence of things from the outside world. These proselytizers bring with them things like furniture, radios, milk packets, dishes, clothes, money, and medicine. As they live with the tribes for many months on end, they work to create homes that mimic their Western lifestyles in order to be comfortable in the midst of the "devil-worshippers" surrounding them. The missionaries then feel sorry for the tribes, not having furniture, not having radios, not having televisions, that they then share these wares amongst them when they leave, enticing the tribes with Western toys, and creating inner tribal conflict. As with the Sawiyanos, they had become lax in traditional forms of entertainment in exchange for static-filled radio and mp3 players on phones. No longer did they create nightly costumes from the bush for sing-sings, or dance with their kundus in hand. When the missionaries leave, these objects are left and spread out through the tribe, usually finding their way to the leader's house (for they are the most greedy within the Sawiyano). Money is also given to the tribe members so that they can travel back and forth between town. This might be the worst charity, as tribe members develop a full expectancy of the missionaries to fund their trips to town. Now mind you, these trips are not cheap! So when the missionaries discover that the tribes are becoming too dependent, they refuse to give any more free rides, and the tribes become upset, refusing to resort to old ways like paddling a canoe to town, when they could instead use a money-costing motor canoe from the missionaries. It has even come to the point that they will refuse to take the motor canoes when they know that they could take an airplane, costing even more money. This sort of dependency from inappropriate handouts will prove to be even more of a problem as the tribes become displaced from their homes.

Similar to the way native tribes of America were treated not so long ago, the tribes of Papua New Guinea are soon facing displacement and destruction. Mining companies have been purchasing mountains from the tribes for mere pennies. In fact, two mountains were sold for $250 each just before our arrival into the tribe. Assuming that history will repeat itself, the rivers of the land will be ruined from the mining process, and eventually, the tribes will have to move on until there is no place but town for survival. This will leave the tribes with problems similar to those of the Native Americans when they were forced to endure life after the tribe. The Language barrier, their continued dependence on the missionaries, lack of ability, sovereignty, and independence will make it increasingly difficult for them to live. It is easy for Westerners to see the problems facing the tribe, because we have made the same mistakes in the past. After talking with the Sawiyano tribe though, they are convinced that their forests will always be with them, that it is impossible for it to disappear, and that there could never be anything wrong with the mining companies. They actually welcome them with open arms as the miners bring jobs and money, *as well as their own personal doctors who find time to treat illnesses inside the tribe. This then brings me to the next point. "What exactly are we supposed to do, or can do, for the tribes of Papua New Guinea once we have become aware? Are they too far removed for us to care? Should it be our responsibility to do something about it? What good is there in discussing these issues?"*

I once read an interview in Sculpture Magazine *with Folkert de Jong titled:* Confronting the Grotesque. *He says, "The weak point in a civilization is its cultural heritage ... Brancusi and Arp were making such minimalistic sculpture at a time when war was raging through much of Europe. I thought, 'How can one possibly make a sculpture of an egg when this is going on?' I was shocked—as an artist, you simply cannot do such a thing. You must take a position. Then, I realized that such reduction and silence in the midst of chaos gives people time to breathe and think about what is essential. I finally understood that the role of the artist is to take a significant position, but that it need not always be an aggressive position. Maybe it's up to the artist to create silence and focus." I think it is appropriate here to replace the word artist with human being. Whether we can help immediately, or adjust our paradigms for the future, we must take a position, understanding that help doesn't simply come in the form of donations or money. There are many other ways in which we can help indigenous tribes.*

If you find yourself actually having the chance to visit these sites, education and awareness are imperative for their continued survival. Education and awareness of medicine, history, reading, writing and a constant reinforcement of their sovereignty will be key as their land is taken from them. It might seem conflicting to teach English literacy, but in order for them to read contracts, and understand these preliminary and post processes, they will need to have these tools for communication. (One might suggest that the mining companies learn the different languages of the tribes, but their concern is elsewhere. As well, having a translator that is the intermediary between the tribes and the companies might help, but this would only weaken the independency of the tribes, and does nothing to help them in being able to help themselves. The key is to provide the tools, and advise them regarding the past that they are unaware of, and thus, unable to have learned from.) But what if you don't have this chance to help out in person?

There are many simple things we can do at home, aside from donations and money. Simply learning and being aware of these issues at hand can assist in the collective conscious that we exist in. The more we educate ourselves and our future generations, the more we will radiate an example of good practice and peace. As Jung mentions, we must learn to take ourselves more seriously. These tribes may be too far removed from our insular locales, but we must care, and at the same time, accept that there are different forms of participation in regards to caring. Our first responsibility is to take care of ourselves, so that we can then take care of others. And part of taking care of others includes letting them take care of you, through new education, and new awareness. It is not a single person's responsibility to take care of these problems, but when the time comes, it will be a collective conscious and effort in helping.

Placing importance on cultural heritage facilitates cultural diversity and regional identity. It also provides regional growth, encourages sustainable development, and strengthens the population. Papua New Guinea could benefit a great deal if they took their own identity more seriously. For it is hard to ignore Port Moresby's airport hallways, where advertisements for mining companies are alongside posters that say "Respect our culture," and, "Respect our flora," with a native tribesman and a hibiscus on each of them respectively. Discussing these issues isn't simply for a passive awareness in ourselves. These concerns are made so that we may have an active conscious, and that through the spread of infection, we can encourage a deeper care for our life-world.

What is our responsibility? Responsibility seems like the wrong term, as if it were hard, individual work. The term scares people away from the bigger issues at hand. How, after all, does a single person really matter? If there are about 6 billion people in this world, and one dies, there are still about 6 billion people in this world. Do not be mistaken though, there is value in life! But what is that value? It's true, it is hard to see your immediate impact on the world, but it is wrong to think like this. We must first look closer, to ourselves, and then to our communities. We cannot rely on mass solutions, as they only reinforce a lack of individual responsibility. We must do the simplest thing, and that is to take ourselves more seriously. We must shift. We must take care of ourselves first, before taking care of others, and in learning how to do so, it is only possible to take care of yourself completely, by letting others help take care of you, and vice versa. This is where value in one life appears, through its interdependencies.

> *"There is only one remedy for the leveling effect of all collective measures, and that is to emphasize and increase the value of the individual … This can only be the business of the individual, and it must begin with the individual in order to be real."*

> *"One must always have something that is good for a hundred thousand, for a million people, but not for the individual, for he is far too uninteresting … And the individual is so utterly convinced of his nothingness that he makes no effort to get anywhere with himself, to develop himself inwardly in any way … It is naturally a false view that the individual is nothing. The individual is the vessel of life. Every individual is the bearer of life."*

> — *Carl Jung*

"We can never pretend to dismiss the adventures of history as something foreign to our present action, since even the most independent search for the most abstract truth has been and is a factor of history ... All human acts and all human creations constitute a single drama, and in this sense we are all saved or lost together. Our life is essentially universal."

— Maurice Merleau-Ponty

We can all see the destruction around us, and yet we wait for it to resolve on its own. Although we might agree, we move on to the next issue. It seems that our own habitat is reinforcing an attitude of self-insulation. We may participate in the organic and local grown scenes, but do we do this for our sensuous world? Or is there a more shallow reason, embedded in social status, and economy? Too many times, the answer seems to start and end with our selves. We must end with the Other and return, and so on. We have muddled our senses with civilization, and now we are stuck deep within it. A deep mud, one that will only set us free if we remove our feet from the boots that suffocate beneath the surface.

The responsibility to react, does not necessarily neglect the responsibility of educating oneself beforehand.

The word compulsion has been coming up in conversations lately, and I find it quite interesting. Much of this book has been written under the influence of compulsion, and the desire to actively/presently speak out. I am compelled to write down my present thoughts. There are consequences to this way of making, or being, and I tend to link other terms with it, like for instance, risk of the action. I also find that some of my previous writings have been edited out of this book due to new awareness and change of thought. Although, they were eventually edited back in for the value that they presented in their time, and might very well present to Others.

Some would say that acting on compulsion would eliminate the foundation of research, or reflection, and in many ways, it can. Some might also use the word intuition, but should be wary not to be confused between the two terms. Intuition is the ability to understand something immediately, without the need for conscious reasoning, while compulsion is an irresistible urge to behave in a certain way, especially against one's conscious wishes. Though, whether intuitively or compelled, there is always time spent before the action no matter how infinitely short or long it may be. I find that when I have time to think, or study, I find reasons not to act. Of course, sometimes there are good reasons for this pre-planning and forgoing of the action, but in many cases, the fact would be learned and realized in both instances. There are different ways for education to happen, and actions bring about knowledge that only actions can bring about. Reading about actions does not educate in the same way that acting out actions does, and vice versa. With acting out, there is a deeper connection, and a kind of participation with every other person who has ever done that action. Perceptions are made, and there is an active step towards empathy and understanding. So as long as one is learning, I think this acting is appropriate. Does reading work in the same way?

I started thinking today about an Armageddon on earth. Not a complete Armageddon, but one that causes lots of fires, and destruction, and death, and an immediate change in the social fabric of our lives, but still, the earth remains, and most of us humans do too. There are no structures to be found as they all have crumbled in the earthquakes, monsoons, and tornadoes. There are no crops left due to the fires that ravaged the land. Nature has been crisped, and it stays hidden away from the humans, knowing not to return for the fear of another great pain. And yet, the humans still survive. They form new tribes. They use the knowledge gained from their lives before the destruction to adapt. And this makes me think of where I would stand.

I am an artist. This is where I've ended up. And while I can build, I am no structural engineer. I am much more invested in the ways of thinking and expressing feeling. And I start to realize how useless my skills are in terms of this post-Armageddon world. Yet, it is one of the only paths that allows you to completely express what it means to be human, and in the midst of these inhumane times, it seems important to do just that. But in doing so seems passive and insular, with no real use for anyone outside of our self. We do this for our own humanness it seems, our own signature, without regard to the rest of humans. And so when I imagine this Armageddon, I see crumbled galleries, and artists who have used movable walls as temporary shelters, vitrines for storing water, and pedestals for fire wood. And I do not see them surviving. I see some that try to warrant peace, others who can't resist their primal urge to create, and others who are simply scared and wishing they had become a banker. Although, who knows how bankers would survive either.

I stopped thinking about this, and realized that most other demographics would probably fare the same way. Surrounding themselves with the things they held dear before the destruction. And this is what scared me most in this thinking, is that we are now, no longer contemporary, in regards to the definition that we no longer think about ideas that are happening now and around us. Instead, we are thinking about ideas that are rooted in the past or future, and inside of us. I speak mainly of professions that are inundated with the idea of becoming famous and rich, or attached to the possibility of being the best, and this includes almost every profession. Even the cubicle farms and fast food restaurants induce strategies that make individuals start thinking about their own performance through reward programs and commission benefits.

Art is a privilege, and as a profession, hasn't exactly proven its worth to the laymen people of the world. Who has time to care about art when you first have to care about the three jobs you have, putting food on the table, and paying last month's bills? And if you never cared in the first place while growing up, it becomes even harder to learn how to care for it now, as art has never proven useful for you in the past. Artists care because that's how they plan to make a living, with or without money. Galleries and museums care because artists make their living for them, with or without money. Yuppies care because the museums throw parties for them to reinforce their status, and in doing so, reinforce art as privilege, and as entertainment, a word rooted in the act of diversion. There might be a few others who care, but would generally be considered extensions of these three.

So then I start to think about how art can become less insular, outside of the self, more useful and of the present, in hopes of surviving.

Before going to Papua New Guinea, I became quite depressed. It might have had something to do with another round of questioning the role of the artist, how I was surviving, and whether or not I was becoming the useful artist I wanted to be. I'm not exactly sure why, but this phenomenon seems to have happened right before going to Ireland as well. The difference being, I had pinned that previous depression down to the fact that I was going to travel abroad, while all of my best friends graduated and moved away. This was resolved as I gained seven of the best friends I could have ever asked for. But why then, did I feel this way before Papua New Guinea? I started to find it hard to experience excitement and joy for the trip. I didn't particularly feel proud of myself, while others were able to tell me so easily that I was doing great. I was a pizza delivery driver, and the only thing I could think of that had come of it, was a new awareness for real life, outside of the forever loving art circle I had once been a part of. I thought the trip would be amazing, and that escaping Minneapolis would feel refreshing. But I thought about coming back, and it didn't seem like that much would have changed. I would be faced once again with paying enormous student loans, and would continue to struggle in finding time to participate in the arts as I searched for another minimum wage job, only to listen to customers complain about how people should try harder, that they should care more. I would reenter a society that doesn't seem to acknowledge its awesome privileges. I thought about joining the Army upon my return. I equated this to giving my life away, or committing suicide. Though, I thought it would be a viable way in which to participate and perceive yet another position that our generation is deeply rooted in. It would be a way to empathize, and to inspire myself. And while I wasn't totally convinced otherwise, there had to be other solutions besides this that would facilitate my growth towards empathy.

I was reminded by my roommate at the time that I am a white North American male. I am part of one of the most innately privileged demographics on the planet. That with this privilege comes a responsibility to do something. But what? She reminded me that simply doing things, and making effort can inspire people. I thought about the kids I worked with, and my own times as a child. What inspired me as a kid, and how seeing things done could set into motion my dreams and goals. Imaginations are rampant, and nothing seems impossible during youth. These impossibilities only start to announce themselves as we grow out of youth. I was in awe during elementary school assemblies, or when guests would present their skills and teach new and exciting lessons. As an adult though, since economy had introduced itself into my life equation, I was having a hard time finding this magic. Like the story of Michael, there have been many times when kids inspired me greatly, reawakening this buried wonder. But these stories are far and in between, unlike the rushing waves of education that happen as a child. I wanted to feel these waves again.

> *"To remain a child too long is childish, but it is just as childish to move away and then assume that childhood no longer exists because we do not see it."*

"We stand on a peak of consciousness, believing in a childish way that the path leads upward to yet higher peaks beyond. That is the chimerical rainbow bridge. In order to reach the next peak we must first go down into the land where the paths begin to divide."

"We are always human, and we should never forget that we carry the whole burden of being only human.."

— Carl Jung

Jung states that we have lost our instinct, but is it just our natural instinct? Does that make any sense? Maybe our instinct has evolved or been traded for a human-made instinct, just as our environment is no longer natural, but is human-made. Our human-made instinct serves us better in our human-made environment than a tribal mans natural instinct can serve him in our built world. Maybe then, it's not a question of loss of instinct, but whether this new instinct is more or less advantageous to us. For it might be helpful to us in a present mode of living but it also distracts us from future consequences. Do we need to experience both to have an awareness of consequence? To learn what each instinct has to offer? There seems to be many different modes of instinct even in America, for the farmer experiences different signified signifiers than the Wall Street banker. Their instincts and modes of survival are extremely different, and yet, still far from this natural instinct that Jung refers to.

I was thinking about Abrams and Jung, and their time spent with tribes and other research, and how long ago these moments existed. The Sawiyano have been severely exposed to modern technology. Their original culture has practically faded. With Christianity, even their myth and ritual is gone. Only the tribe members who have not converted to Christianity will partake in traditional Tumbuna culture, as their funerals will consist of the old way. By then, it is too late. Other than billums, their traditional woven bags, not much else remains. Even their hunting tools have nails, or rubber to keep them working. Even though they still rely on nature to survive, technology has penetrated their forms of entertainment, clothing, myth, and ritual; almost every aspect of their lives. They simply aren't the tribe they were twenty years ago. When you read about things of this nature, you're reading into the past, i.e. how great some schools may be, how a culture is; stigmas are formed over time and only those who are lucky enough to be in those moments will know them for their true nature. By the time we hear about them, they may have changed. Last year was so last year, but what about this year? With social media, does this information become more accessible, and at faster rates? How will stigma function in the future?

Writing has the tendency to exoticize, even if it is non-fictional, as our minds tend to exaggerate and are unable to create the full and true experience that writing tries to offer. Just as the audience in the art world formulates their own thoughts, readers create their own worlds inside of their heads when reading. Thus, a book that tries to share reflections and lived experiences might fail in this sense, as the reader inevitably creates their own inside of their head. The advantage to this is that readers tend to connect their own past experiences to ones in the book and start to form a relationship with the overall being that the book is derived from, creating a stronger discussion between the book and its reader. To note, pictures can help dissipate this aforementioned exoticism, but as our eyes don't see without our noses smelling, our mouths tasting, our feet touching, and our ears listening, the book still remains far from the lived experience. So if anything, I would hope that writing can inspire an eagerness to experience, connect, and think in new ways.

We, especially young people, live in a culture of immediacy. This wasn't made clear to me until my travels abroad, but the United States of America, even at its lowest levels, is one of, if not the most, privileged nations in the world. And still, I meet people, mostly younger, who think of themselves as non-privileged. This is, of course, based on the individuals' own experiences and perspectives of life around them, and is just another reason to argue the goodness of travel. We all tend to want something more in life, whether it be possessions, a new job in our desired field, or a steady relationship. We grow up with the assumption that we will have a job, make money, be successful. Everyone gets asked, "what do you want to be when you grow up?" And when we don't get these things right away, we become impatient, upset, and have thoughts of giving up, wanting to leave our childhood dreams behind. It doesn't take long in this age of immediacy for our impatience to take over when something takes longer than a couple months to attain. I myself, am guilty of this impatience.

When I graduated from college, I was extremely fortunate to have the opportunity to travel to Beijing, China for a teaching residency. My loan payments wouldn't be kicking in until six months after graduation, and the residency was only three months long. I figured that with my experience in Beijing, I would either find work abroad, or come back and be even more valuable to possible employers. I was right. When I came back, there were several positions open for community arts education and direction. I applied and received an interview for each one. I felt like everything was falling into place. Though, when it came time for the interview, and I met the people who were on the panels, the good energy came to a halt. Despite my experience in Beijing, and eight years previous of working with public schools, I was still a twenty-two year old, and half the age of every one of their staff members. Each interview was conducted, and each one ended the same, with a comment on my age and the political ramifications of hiring me. When I met other program directors, it seemed I would need to wait at least another decade until I would be considered "old enough."

With only a month left until my loans kicked in, I continued to bide time as a gardener, gallery assistant, after school art teacher, and free-lance art technician. I kept watching the weekly job boards, but the vast pool of Autumn jobs was evaporating. On the week of my first loan payment, I still didn't have a consistent job, and with the help of a friend, was introduced to delivering pizza.

This job as a pizza delivery driver was maybe one of the worst, and best things, to ever happen to me. I was faced with a community of workers and customers completely outside of the insular art realm, and I was introduced to amazing "real-life" revelations. The work wasn't hard per se, but it caused a mental atrophy, or so it seemed, as I was surrounded by activity that wasn't facilitating the kind of critical thought I wanted to be having. After several months, I became content with working 60 hours a week, and checking the job boards in my spare time. At the least, through its distance from my pursuits, the job did inspire me to become even hungrier for art working. If pizza delivery had instead been a 40 hour per week office job with higher pay, would I have become content to leave my passion for the arts? Eventually though, I realized it would be easier to make my own opportunities, rather than relying on employers. This is when I was reintroduced to Bethany Kalk, and the opportunity travel to Papua New Guinea. Though, it seemed I still couldn't escape the ironic sides of life.

During my initial stages of fundraising for the trip to Papua New Guinea, a position opened up at a nearby college to run their sculpture lab. It seemed like the world was teasing me with two great opportunities. I decided to apply, even though I knew the position start date was the day I left for the island with Bethany. After letting the interview panel know about my travel intentions, I knew it was another failed interview. I was told to always take once-in-a-lifetime opportunities, because if someone really wants you, they will wait for you to come back. Unfortunately, this wasn't the case, and the school hired somebody else. I was a little disappointed, but not horribly so, because I was right back where I was, with an amazing trip to Papua New Guinea, and enough money saved up to last me three months back on arrival to search out another job. I was done with pizza.

The trip was amazing, and upon my coming back to the states, I found that finding a new job was quite easy. It was the season for students to return to school and restaurants were hiring fast. I became a chef at an upscale pizza kitchen, and was then offered the assistant managing position at a family-owned restaurant that I had been great friends with all through college. I was excited to apply for grants, and new artist opportunities, and start off on a clean slate. The previous year, being the first after school, was complete misery. As soon as I accepted the assistant managing position, I got a call from the school with the sculpture lab position I had previously interviewed with. Surprised, and on my bike in the middle of downtown Minneapolis, I was asked if I was still interested in the job. The position had become open again. I re-interviewed a few days later, was offered the position, and moved out of town two days after that. It was a whirlwind return, and nothing I could have ever expected, which seems to be the moral here.

Almost everything I have applied for after school by myself, I haven't gotten. There is a formula of goal plus completion equals success, and by not completing these goals, we instead get failure as an answer. Though, the things I have succeeded in doing, are all opportunities that simply came to me out of the blue. I stayed involved through discussions with friends, taking on more projects than seemed possible, and advising friends with their new projects. Through this involvement, I was called for teaching jobs at local public school programs, I was reconnected with Bethany for the chance to go to Papua New Guinea, and even several offers to create and show new work in institutional spaces. This offer for the sculpture lab seemed no different. I failed in getting it the first time, and could only attain it through being given it after the fact. It is a hard lesson to stay a believer in, but requires a major paradigm shift. We typically won't get everything we want right away, and maybe won't ever get anything that we set out for. Though, by staying involved with a community and working hard in all things, the world seems to recognize your talent and place you at its own pace. Our society is human-made, and so too is our culture of immediacy. Nature itself will never coincide with this immediacy. Its pace cannot be forced into something so man-made, and when that effort is made, it usually backfires with the destruction of wildlife, food supplies, river systems, indigenous tribes, the earth's atmosphere, and much more. If we look for the easy way out, we will eventually pay for it later on. We must act more in line with the earth, and be in the world with a more natural pace. We must understand our privilege and place in the world by learning from Others. We must stay involved, be patient and open. We must actively wait with our porch lights on, and our candy bowls full, ready to treat the opportunities that come knocking.

My job as a pizza delivery driver gave me the allowance of day-dreaming quite a bit at work. I would fall into the patterns of the road, not quite seeing where I was going, but knowing where it was that I would end up. Yi-Fu Tuan talks about this in *Space and Place*, referring to the idea that we pass through spaces, to end up at places. When I drive, I also listen to Top 40s. In some way, these songs provide a pace, but in other ways, allow me to be even more thoughtful, due to their lack of substance.

For instance, as I drove back to the shop one day I came to a red light and looked out my window to see the Minneapolis skyline. And to note, there are quite a few intersections that provide great glances into the architectural life of the city, and are only made visible to the people who have spent so much time driving in between these giants to remember to look up and around. In any case though, on this occasion I looked out and directly next to me was a small patch of dead land, a section of chain link fence, and a single chirping bird. I became quite interested in the creature, wondering how exactly it got there, where its home was, and why it was chirping all alone. Was it calling for its friends or family, sending out a call, or did it see myself, in my truck, and think that I was something to be calling out to? To make sure, I scanned the rest of the landscape but could not see any other life, or at least, life that could make out such audible calls to my human ears like that of a bird, or a car.

This bird made me think about the times I have been alone, away from home, and surrounded by a foreign landscape. In Rotterdam I talked to myself at times to keep motivated, while in Ireland I couldn't help but to cry out in joy, for the landscape sung beautifully and I had to respond. Beijing may be most relevant here, in that when we spoke, we could not understand each other, and this language barrier also existed between the bird and myself. But something was in fact being communicated here between us. Like in Beijing, some context of the situation would hint at the meaning, left up for assumption. I would speak in English, or broken Mandarin and point at pictures of what I wanted. And because I was in a restaurant, it was known that I would want to eat this or that. The look on my face, the speed at which I spoke, the gestures that my hands made, and the way I walked about could all signify meaning.

For the bird, it sat on a fence, overlooking a street to one side, and the city skyline on the other. The wind was somewhere else at the moment, and distant sounds of cars and city life could be heard at this edge of the urban perimeter. Sitting alone, atop a small patch of dead grass, the bird turned its head quickly, maybe doing a few hops, and observed the world. A large gray truck approaches, loud and reeking of gasoline and pizza. Besides these sounds, the truck is also making it's own voice with the help of the local 80s love-pop radio station. An intruder to the seemingly calm scene, the bird sees the truck pull to a stop and looks at the human behind the wheel, or maybe not even recognizing it as a human, for the human has become melded with this automobile, and in turn, has become a new creature that all animals see as an extension of our species. Either way, the bird looks up and starts to chirp. It chirps at the truck and then faces out and chirps into the wind that has returned. Maybe it feels threatened, or scared, or maybe some high pitch noise of the radio is communicating something that beckons response. Left to the unknown, the light turns green and the truck storms back to work.

The leader of the Wapualu tribe, Bob Mera, tells a story about two friends, a monkey and a shark.

There was once a monkey and a shark who were very good friends. They always played together along the seashore. One day, the shark told the monkey that his dad was very sick and that they should go visit him. Knowing that they were good friends and the monkey had never seen the shark's dad he agreed to hop on top of the shark's back and swim out to his home. After traveling out to sea and unable to see land, they finally reached his home. The shark turned around to the monkey and said, "Monkey, my dad is very sick." Monkey knew this, and then Shark said, "the only way he can get better is if you give him your liver." Monkey was shocked and knew that if he gave his liver to the shark he would die, but if he said no, the shark would surely take it because he was so far from his home and couldn't escape. So Monkey replied calmly, "Oh Shark, I'm sorry. I will gladly give you my liver, but I left it at home. We must go back to get it." Shark replied, "Oh, thank you Monkey, you are a true friend. I will take you back home so you can get your liver." So Shark turned around and swam back to Monkey's home. As they came to shore, Monkey told Shark to wait in the water as he climbed up to his home in a very tall coconut tree. Once on top and out of Shark's reach, Monkey called out to Shark, "Oh friend, I'm sorry I tricked you, but my liver is inside of me and you can't have it." Monkey laughed and danced about as Shark swam away angrily.

In this story, Bob explains, we are the monkey, and we all are friends with evil spirits, or sharks. We play with them all the time, but sometimes they lead us into a very dangerous position. We must choose to either fall into temptation or escape. Escaping is very easy, as it is up to us to make the choice.

Before this trip, I've been reading works from philosophers who have spent time with indigenous tribes. I can't quite grasp whether they really ever spent significant time with the tribes. In their works, they seem to only ever be observers. They describe the actions that the tribes do themselves, but not what they did together with the author. I wonder if Jung ever laughed and danced with a tribe, or if Abram ever sang along with tribal songs. They must have. How could they have not? I wonder if these are things I will get to do. I have heard that the kids love soccer.

Of course they loved soccer.

And of course I got blisters from playing barefoot.

But only on the soft spots.

IMPORTANT QUOTES

When I look through bibliographies, I discover references that would have been helpful in reading beforehand. These are quotes from books and articles that I read while attempting to write my own. I struggled with whether or not to keep this section, but I find them helpful with regards to the bibliography. They were a strong influence for me, and provide a good reference to my thoughts and concerns. I hope you find relation to them as well, whether now, or some time later, upon the road we walk.

"We tried to think about the most primitive information we have regarding our extraordinary experience, is that, I think we choose the fact that, all humanity has always been born naked, absolutely helpless, for months, and though with beautiful equipment, as we learn later on, with no experience, and therefore, absolutely ignorant. That's where all humanity has always started. And we've come to the point where, in our trial and error finding our way, stimulated by a designed in hunger designed in thirst these are conscious inputs; designed in procreative urge we have such an enormous amount of, as we learn later on, of designed in automated processing of the inter-relationships of all the atoms in our organism, starting then, with a consciousness of the hunger, giving a drive to go after... to seek to experiment. Man having, then, no rule book, nothing to tell him about that Universe, has had to really find his way entirely by trial and error. He had no words and no experience to assume that the other person has experience. The at first, very incredibly limited way of communicating. We now know, human beings being on our planet for probably 3 1/2 million years, with, as far as we can see, not much physiological change, pretty much the same skeleton, and from what we can learn of human beings in their earliest recorded communicating, in an important degree, people in India 5,000 years ago, and in China 5,000 years ago, were thinking very extraordinarily well in the terms of anything we know about our experience, the way we've been able to resolve experiences into the discovery of principles that seem to be operative in our Universe."

— Buckminster Fuller

"There are many ways to create inventions. My way is to dive under the water. Too much oxygen is bad for the brain, on the other hand, if the brain feels a shortage of oxygen, brain feels it. Then the brain reaches maximum activity, 0.5 seconds before death. Then I can suddenly create a breakthrough, a new idea. An idea comes instantly and disappears instantly. (...) As close as to the death as possible, that is important. So I do my inventing balancing death and invention."

— Yoshiro Nakamatsu

"All my knowledge of the world, even my scientific knowledge, is gained from my own particular point of view, or from some experience of the world without which the symbols of science would be meaningless. The whole universe of science is built upon the world as directly experienced, and if we want to subject science itself to rigorous scrutiny and arrive at a precise assessment of its meaning and scope, we must begin by reawakening the basic experience of the world of which science is the second-order expression. (...) To return to things themselves is to return to that world which precedes knowledge, of which knowledge always speaks, and in relation to which every scientific schematization is an abstract and derivative sign-language, as is geography in relation to the country-side in which we have learnt beforehand what a forest, a prairie or a river is."

"In so far as my hand knows hardness and softness, and my gaze knows the moon's light, it is as a certain way of linking up the phenomena and communicating with it. Hardness and softness, roughness and smoothness, moonlight and sunlight, present themselves in our recollection not pre-eminently as sensory contents but as certain kinds of symbioses, certain ways the outside has of invading us and certain ways we have of meeting this invasion."

"By these words, 'the primacy of perception,' we mean that the experience of perception is our presence at the moment when things, truths, values are constituted for us ..."

"The perceived life-world is the primary reality."

"The characteristic operation of the mind is in the movement by which we recapture our corporeal existence and use it to symbolize instead of merely to coexist."

"When a writer is no longer capable of thus founding a new universality and of taking the risk of communicating, he has outlived his time. It seems to me that we can also say of other institutions that they have ceased to live when they show themselves incapable of carrying on a poetry of human relations—that is, the call of each individual freedom to all the others."

"Perception does not give me truths like geometry but presences."

"If I consider … the problem of knowing how my experience is related to the experience which others have of the same objects, perception will again appear as the paradoxical phenomenon which renders being accessible to us."

"Our certainty about perceiving a given thing does not guarantee that our experience will not be contradicted, or dispense us from a fuller experience of that thing. Naturally it is necessary to establish here a difference between ideal truth and perceived truth."

"What saves us is the possibility of a new development, and our power of making even what is false, true—by thinking through our errors and replacing them within the domain of truth."

"We also live in the imaginary, also in the world of ideality. Thus it is necessary to develop a theory of imaginary existence and of ideal existence."

"The man who philosophizes believes wrongly that when he thinks and affirms he is only expressing the mute contact of his thought with his thought. He is wrong to proceed as if he were not linked to the surrounding circumstances."

"The first result of reflection is to bring us back into the presence of the world as we lived before our reflection began."

"In order to understand truly what has been discovered about man, we must, therefore, combine induction with the reflective knowledge that we can obtain from ourselves as conscious subjects."

— Maurice Merleau-Ponty

"We thereby recognize that our own future happiness and welfare is dependent on the many other members of our society."

— The Dalai Lama

"In the future we will establish radical relationships with our surroundings. The global becomes the local. Everywhere is a portal to anywhere else. Leaving the notion of place, questioning its identity, in a database of possible environments."

— Paul Nicholls, Factory Fifteen

"When I saw the garden at Ryoanji, I thought: it makes the flow of the stream into an image (...) you have to sit still to contemplate the motion of a stream. Perhaps also to observe one's thoughts. And sitting still is a privilege of peace."

"When she paints (or I write), the mind wanders—if you are afraid of where it might wander, you don't paint (or write)."

"Why any page at all. Why add. What wisdom it would be, not to write. (...) I realize now why I am writing to you: I feel unfit to tell this story. But I have been cast in the role regardless."

— Damon Krukowski

"The maintenance of a site requires both physical caring— for example the rubbing of rocks or clearing of debris—and the performance of (ritual) items aimed at caring for the spirit housed at it. Without these maintenance processes the site remains, but it is said to lose the spirit housed within it. It is then said to die and all those who share physical features and spiritual connections with it are then also thought to die. Thus, to endure the well-being of life, sites must be cared for and rites performed to keep alive the dreaming powers entrapped within them."

— Helen Payne

"We must stand apart from the conventions of history, even while using the record of the past, for the idea of history is itself a western invention whose central theme is the rejection of habitat. It formulates experience outside of nature and tends to reduce place only to a stage upon which the human drama is enacted. History conceives the past mainly in terms of biography and nations. It seeks causality in the conscious, spiritual, ambitious character of men and memorializes them in writing."

— Paul Shepard

"The purpose in running was to remake the time of the world, giving it a pace, to embody the distances, colonizing them with visions from below, bit by bit, but continuously, in sequence, as if only the body were the plot, the narrative thread that could describe the world and its variety."

"To be contemporary would signify today taking imminent catastrophes seriously: the slumification of the world, the end of the city through the depletion of resources, the question of survival, of a human cohabitation that takes into account a sustainable environment, with a redistribution of opportunities for access to resources; it would mean adapting ourselves in every way to avoid the entire city's becoming a battlefield torn among ethnicities, forces, gangs, and crazed subjectivity."

— Franco La Cecla

"Matter in the wrong place is dirt. People got dirty through too much civilization. Whenever we touch nature, we get clean."

"I once experienced a violent earthquake, and my first, immediate feeling was that I no longer stood on solid familiar earth, but on the skin of a gigantic animal that was heaving under my feet. It was this image that impressed itself on me, not the physical fact."

"Enchantment is the oldest form of medicine."

"I see the suffering of mankind in the individual and vice versa."

"We are awakening a little to the feeling that something is wrong in the world, that our modern prejudice or overestimating the importance of the intellect and the conscious mind might be false. We want simplicity. We are suffering, in our cities, from a need of simple things. We would like to see our great ... terminals deserted, the streets deserted, a great peace descend upon us."

"Americans tend(ed) to think in great abstractions and emphasize control over emotions and instincts; and how prevalent was the illusion that anyone could become anything they wished ... Americans need to rest a while and realize that the things being sought are irrelevant to a happy life."

"Man... is a top animal exiled on a tiny speck of a planet in the Milky Way. That is the reason why he does not know himself; he is cosmically isolated. He can only state with certainty that he is no monkey, no bird, no fish, and no tree. But what he positively is, remains obscure."

"Modern man believes that he can do as he pleases and is perturbed that inexplicable anxieties plague him."

"Are we not the carriers of the entire history of mankind?"

"There is no H-bomb in nature."

"I have done without electricity, and tend the fireplace and stove myself. Evenings, I light the old lamps. There is no running water, and I pump the water from the well. I chop the wood and cook the food. These simple acts make man simple; and how difficult it is to be simple!"

"The more uncertain I have felt about myself, the more there has grown up in me a feeling of kinship with all things."

" ... an ideal potentiality of life has become reality (in America)."

"One never knows which is more enjoyable: catching sight of new shores, or discovering new approaches to age-old knowledge that has been almost forgotten."

"Anyone who fails to go along with life remains suspended, stiff and rigid in midair. That is why so many people get wooden in old age; they look back and cling to the past with a secret fear of death in their hearts. They withdraw from the life process, at least psychologically, and consequently remain fixed like nostalgic pillars of salt, with vivid recollections of youth but no living relation to the present."

"To explain certain thinking processes in a modern man, one cannot get along today without the past."

"Man's advance toward the Logos was a great achievement, but he must pay for it with a loss of instinct and loss of reality to the degree that he remains in primitive dependence on mere words."

"The psychic life of civilized man, however, is full of problems; we cannot even think of it except in terms of problems. Our psychic processes are made up to a large extent of reflections, doubts, experiments, all of which are almost completely foreign to the unconscious, instinctive mind of primitive man."

" ... loss of roots ... is a disaster not only for primitive tribes, but for civilized man as well ... The life of instinct—the most conservative element in man—always expresses itself in traditional usages. Age-old convictions and customs are always deeply rooted in the instincts. If they get lost, the conscious mind becomes severed from the instincts and loses its roots, while the instincts, unable to express themselves, fall back into the unconscious and reinforce its energy, causing this in turn to overflow into the existing contents of consciousness. It is then that the rootless condition of consciousness becomes a real danger. This secret vis-a-tergo results in a hybrid of the conscious mind which manifests in the form of exaggerated self-esteem or an inferiority complex. At all levels a loss of balance ensues, and this is the most fruitful soil for psychic injury."

"For it is the body, the feeling, the instincts, which connect us with the soil. If you give up the past you naturally detach from the past; you lose your roots in the soil, your connection with the totem ancestors that dwell in your soil. You turn outward and drift away, and try to conquer other lands because you are exiled from your own soil. That is inevitable. The feet will walk away and the head cannot retain them because it also is looking out for something. That is the Will, always wandering over the surface of the earth, always seeking something. It is exactly what Mountain Lake, the Pueblo Chief, said to me, 'The Americans are quite crazy. They are always seeking; we don't know what they are looking for.' Well, there is too much head and so there is too much will, too much walking about, and nothing rooted."

"People speak of belief when they have lost knowledge ... The naive primitive doesn't believe, he knows, because the inner experience rightly means as much to him as the outer."

"In that world, man is far more exposed to accidents than we are in our sheltered and well-regulated existence. When you are in the bush you dare not take too many chances. The European soon comes to appreciate this."

"When I am not in full control of myself, I am hampered in my movements, my attention wanders, I get absent minded. As a result I knock against something, stumble, drop something, forget something. Under civilized conditions, these are mere trifles, but in the primeval forest they mean mortal danger. I make a false step on a slippery tree-trunk that serves as a bridge over a river teeming with crocodiles. I lose my compass in the high grass. I forget to load my rifle and blunder into a rhinoceros trail in the jungle. I am preoccupied with my thoughts and step on a puff-adder. At nightfall I forget to put on my mosquito-boots in time and eleven days later I die from an onset of tropical malaria. To forget to keep one's mouth shut while bathing is enough to bring on a fatal attack of dysentery."

"Our intellect has created a new world that dominates nature, and has populated it with monstrous machines. The latter are so indubitably useful and so much needed that we cannot see even a possibility of getting rid of them or of our odious subservience to them."

"In spite of our proud domination of nature we are still her victims as much as ever and have not even learnt to control our own nature, which slowly and inevitably courts disaster."

"We rid the world of malaria, we spread hygiene everywhere, with the result that under-developed populations increase at such a rate that food is becoming a problem. 'We have conquered nature' is a mere slogan."

"The man whose interests are all outside is never satisfied with what is necessary, but is perpetually hankering after something more and better which, true to his bias, he always seeks outside himself. He forgets completely that, for all his outward successes, he himself remains the same inwardly, and he therefore laments his poverty if he possesses only one automobile when the majority have two. Obviously the outward lives of men could do with a lot more bettering and beautifying, but these things lose their meaning when the inner man does not keep pace with them."

"The power of science and technics in Europe is so enormous and indisputable that there is little point in reckoning up all that can be done and all that has been invented. One shudders at the stupendous possibilities. Quite another question begins to loom up: Who is applying for this technical skill? In whose hands does this power lie? For the present, the state is a provisional means of protection, because, apparently, it safeguards the citizen from the enormous quantities of poison gas and other infernal engines of destruction which can be manufactured by the thousand tons at a moment's notice. Our technical skill has grown to be so dangerous that the most urgent question today is not what more can be done in this line, but how the man who is entrusted with the control of this skill should be constituted, or how to alter the mind of Western man so that he would renounce his terrible skill. It is infinitely more important to strip him of the illusion of his power than to strengthen him still further in the mistaken idea that he can do everything he wills."

"People still do not know that the greatest step forward is balanced by an equally great step back."

"No one has yet become a good surgeon by learning the textbooks by heart. Yet the danger that faces us today is that the whole of reality will be replaced by words. This accounts for that terrible lack of instinct in modern man, particularly the city-dweller. He lacks all contact with life and the breath of nature. He knows a rabbit or a cow from an illustrated paper, the dictionary, or the movies, and thinks he knows what it is really like—and then is amazed that cow sheds 'smell' because the dictionary didn't say so."

"All time-saving devices … do not, paradoxically enough, save us time, but merely cram our time so full that we have no time for anything."

"If one views modern art prospectively, as I think one can, it plainly announces the uprush of the dissolvent forces of disorder. It clears the air by abolishing the constraints of order."

"The deviation from the [archetypal] dominants causes a certain dissociation, i.e., a loss of vitality, what the primitives call a 'loss of soul.' The primitive has a very keen realization in this respect. I would mention the story of the native [African] who had been invited to be driven in a car. After half an hour he asked the people to stop. He stepped out and stretched himself on the ground. They asked him whether he was sick, and he said, 'no,' he felt alright, but he had just to wait for his soul that had remained behind, as they went too fast for it. I had to think of my American visitors who fly over here in six hours and are still in America for several days, without noticing it."

"Nobody can tell me that man feels like a king in New York. He is just an ant on an ant heap and doesn't count at all, he is superfluous there, the ant heap is the thing that counts. It is a town which should be inhabited by giants; then I would believe that those buildings belonged to them."

"In general it can be said that for modern man, technology is an imbalance that begets dissatisfaction with work or with life. It estranges man from his natural versatility of action and thus allows many of his instincts to lie fallow. The result is an increased resistance to work in general."

"In earlier times, when the crafts flourished, (the worker) derived satisfaction from seeing the fruit of his labor. He found adequate self-expression in such work. But this is no longer the case."

"Everything surrounding me is part of me, and that is precisely why a rented apartment is disastrous. It offers so few possibilities for self-expression. In a standardized apartment, in a standardized milieu, it is easy to lose the sense of one's own personality, of one's individuality."

"Noise, like crowds, gives a feeling of security; therefore people love it and avoid doing anything about it as they instinctively feel the apotropaic magic it sends out. Noise protects us from painful reflection."

"We have no standpoint outside of the human sphere. Thus we don't know what man is. We can only say that he is no animal, nor a plant, nor a crystal, but what he is is impossible to say. We would need an intimate knowledge of the inhabitants of other planets, inasmuch as they can be compared with men, in order to enable us to form some idea of what man is."

"Everyone thinks that psychology is what he himself knows best—physiology is always his psychology, which he alone knows, and at the time his psychology is everybody else's psychology. Instinctively he supposes that his own psychic constitution is the general one, and that everyone is essentially like everyone else, that is to say, like himself ... as though his own psyche were a kind of master-psyche which suited all and sundry, and entitled him to suppose that his own situation was the general rule. People are profoundly astonished, or even horrified, when this rule quite obviously does not fit—when they discover that another person really is different from themselves."

"This primitive reaction survives in us too: how prompt we are to make offense when somebody does not share our convictions! We are insulted when somebody finds our ideas of beauty detestable. We still persecute anyone who thinks differently from ourselves, we still try to force our opinions on others, to convert poor heathens in order to save them from the hell that indubitably lies in wait for them, and we are all abysmally afraid of standing alone with our beliefs."

"For primitive egoism, however, the standing rule is that it is never 'I' who must change, but always the other fellow."

"If we are honest, we must admit that no one feels quite comfortable in the present-day world; indeed, it becomes increasingly uncomfortable. The word 'crisis,' so often heard, is a medical expression which always tells us that the sickness has reached a dangerous climax."

"This knowledge, furthermore, should not be dead material that has been memorized; it must possess a living quality, and be infused with the experience of the person who uses it. Of what use is philosophical knowledge in the head, if one is not also a philosopher at heart? ... for nowhere can he see anything more than what he is himself."

"Whenever we touch nature we get clean. Savages are not dirty— only we are dirty."

"When we must deal with problems, we instinctively refuse to try the way that leads through darkness and obscurity. We wish to hear only equivocal results, and completely forget that these results can only be brought about when we have ventured into and emerged again from the darkness."

"In our time, it's the intellect that is making darkness, because we've let it take too big a place. Consciousness discriminates, judges, analyzes, and emphasizes the contradictions. It's necessary work up to a point. But analysis kills and synthesis brings to life. We must find out how to get everything back into connection with everything else. We must resist the vice of intellectualism, and get it understood that we cannot only understand."

"If one has the right attitude, then the right things happen."

"So the best cure for anybody is when the one who thinks about curing has cured himself ... if he is in Tao, he has established Tao, and whoever beholds him beholds Tao and enters Tao. This is a very Eastern idea. The Western idea—particularly late Christianity— is of course to cure your neighbor, to help him, with no consideration of the question, 'Who is the helper?'"

"One needs faith, courage, and no end of honesty and patience."

— Carl Jung

"Direct sensuous reality, in all its more-than-human mystery, remains the sole solid touchstone for an experiential world now inundated with electronically-generated vistas and engineered pleasures; only in regular contact with the tangible ground and sky can we learn how to orient and to navigate in the multiple dimensions that now claim us."

"As humans, we are well acquainted with the needs and capacities of the human body—we *live* our own bodies and so know, from within, the possibilities of our form. We cannot know, with the same familiarity and intimacy, the lived experience of a grass snake or a snapping turtle; we cannot readily experience the precise sensations of a hummingbird sipping nectar from a flower or a rubber tree soaking up sunlight."

"If the relative attunement to environing nature exhibited by native cultures is linked to a more primordial, participatory mode of perception, how had Western civilization come to be so exempt from this sensory reciprocity? How, that is, have we become so deaf and so blind to the vital existence of other species, and to the animate landscapes they inhabit, that we now so casually bring about their destruction?"

"It is this informing of my perceptions by the evident perceptions and sensations of other bodily entities that establishes, for me, the relative solidity and stability of the world."

(Regarding Merleau-Ponty and phenomenology)

"A philosophy that would strive, not to explain the world from the outside, but to give voice to the world from our experienced situation *within* it, recalling us to our participation in the here-and-now, rejuvenating our sense of wonder at the fathomless things, events and powers that surround us on every hand."

"The relative divergence of my bodily senses (eyes in the front of the head, ears towards the back, etc.) and their curious bifurcation (not one but *two* eyes, one on each side, and similarly two ears, two nostrils, etc.), indicates that this body is a form destined to the world; it ensures that my body is a sort of open circuit that completes itself only in things, in others, in the encompassing earth."

"If the surroundings are experienced as sensate, attentive, and watchful, then I must take care that my actions are mindful and respectful, even when I am far away from other humans, lest I offend the watchful land itself."

"In indigenous, oral cultures, in other words, language seems to encourage and augment the participatory life of the sense, while in Western civilization, language seems to deny or deaden that life, promoting a massive distrust or sensorial experience while valorizing an abstract realm of ideas hidden behind or beyond the sensory appearances."

"Words like 'rush,' 'splash,' 'gush,' 'wash.' For the sound that unites all theses words is that which the water itself chants as it flows between the banks."

"We have at last come to realize that neither the soils, the oceans, nor the atmosphere can be comprehended without taking into account the participation of innumerable organisms, from the lichens that crumble rocks, and the bacterial entities that decompose organic detritus, to all the respiring plants and animals exchanging vital gases with the air."

"As technological civilization diminishes the biotic diversity of the earth, language itself is diminished. As there are fewer and fewer songbirds in the air, due to the destruction of their forests and wetlands, human speech loses more and more of its evocative power. For when we no longer hear the voices of warbler and wren, our own speaking can no longer be nourished by their cadences. As the splashing speech of the rivers is silenced by more and more dams, as we drive more and more of the land's wild voices into the oblivion of extinction, our own languages become increasingly impoverished and weightless, progressively emptied of their earthly resonance."

(Regarding Plato)

"He had strong reservations about the written word and its ability to convey the full meaning of a philosophy that was as much a practice—involving direct personal interaction and instruction— as it was a set of static formulations and reflections. Writing, according to Socrates, can at best serve as a reminder to a reader who already knows those things that have been written."

"To directly perceive any phenomenon is to enter into relation with it, to feel oneself in a living interaction with another being."

"It should be easy, now, to understand the destitution of indigenous, oral persons who have been forcibly displaced from their traditional lands. The local earth is, for them, the very matrix of discursive meaning; to force them from their native ecology (for whatever political or economic purpose) is to render them speechless— or to render their speech meaningless—*to dislodge them from the very ground of coherence*. It is, quite simply, to force them out of their mind. The massive 'relocation' or 'transmigration' projects underway in numerous parts of the world today in the name of 'progress' (for example, the forced 'relocation' of oral peoples in Indonesia and Malaysia in order to make way for the commercial clearcutting of their forests) must be understood, in this light, as instances of cultural genocide."

"Intelligence is no longer ours alone but is a property of the earth; we are in it, of it, immersed in its depths. And indeed each terrain, each ecology, seems to have its own particular intelligence, its unique vernacular of soil and leaf and sky."

"By denying that birds and other animals have their own styles of speech, by insisting that the river has no real voice and that the ground itself is mute, we stifle our direct experience. We cut ourselves off from the deep meanings in many of our words, severing our language from that which supports and sustains it. We then wonder why we are often unable to communicate even among ourselves."

"Is there not something terrifically valuable about the modern faith in human equality? Although achieved at the cost of our cultural attunement to the particular places we inhabit, is there not something wondrous about the spreading recognition that we are part of a single, unitary earth?

Perhaps there is. And yet it is a precarious value. For at the very moment that human populations on every continent have come to recognize the planet as a unified whole, we discover that so many other species are rapidly dwindling and vanishing, that the rivers are choking from industrial wastes, that the sky itself is wounded. At the very moment that the idea of human equality has finally spread, via the printed word or the electronic media, into every nation, it becomes apparent that it is indeed nothing more than an idea, that in some of the most 'developed' of nations humans are nevertheless destroying each other, physically and emotionally, in unprecedented numbers—whether through warfare, through the callousness of corporate greed, or through a rapidly spreading indifference.

Clearly, something is terribly missing, some essential ingredient has been neglected, some necessary aspect of life has been dangerously overlooked, set aside, or simply forgotten in the rush toward a common world. In order to obtain the astonishing and unifying image of the whole earth whirling in the darkness of space, human, it would seem, have had to relinquish something just as valuable—the humility and grace that comes from being fully a part of the whirling world. We have forgotten the poise that comes from living in storied relation and reciprocity with the myriad things, the myriad *beings*, that perceptually surround us.

Only if we can renew that reciprocity—grounding our newfound capacity for literate abstraction in those older, oral forms of experience—only then will the abstract intellect find its real value. It is surely no matter of 'going back,' but rather of coming full circle, uniting our capacity for cool reason with those more sensorial and mimetic ways of knowing, letting the vision of a common world root itself in our direct, participatory engagement with the local and the particular. If, however, we simply persist in our reflective cocoon, then all of our abstract ideals and aspirations for a unitary world will prove horribly delusory. If we do not soon remember ourselves to our sensuous surroundings, if we do not reclaim our solidarity with the other sensibilities that inhabit and constitute those surroundings, then the cost of our human commonality may be our common extinction."

"A genuinely ecological approach does not work to attain a mentally envisioned future, but strives to enter, ever more deeply, into the sensorial present."

"But what then of writing? (...) For those of us who care for an earth not encompassed by machines, a world of textures, tastes, and sounds other than those that we have engineered, there can be no question of simply abandoning literacy, of turning away from all writing. Our task, rather, is that of *taking up* the written word, with all of its potency, and patiently, carefully, writing language back into the land. Our craft is that of releasing the budded, earthly intelligence of our words, freeing them to respond to the speech of the things themselves—to the green uttering-forth of leaves from the spring branches. It is the practice of spinning stories that have the rhythm and lilt of the local soundscape, tales for the tongue, tales that want to be told, again and again, sliding off the digital screen and slipping off the lettered page to inhabit these coastal forests, those desert canyons, those whispering grasslands and valleys and swamps. Finding phrases that place us in contact with the trembling neck-muscles of a deer holding its antlers high as it swims toward the mainland, or with the ant dragging a scavenged rice-grain through the grasses. Planting words, like seeds, under rocks and fallen logs—letting language take root, once again, in the earthen silence of shadow and bone and leaf."

— David Abram

ABOUT THE AUTHOR

Brian Nigus is a Milwaukee-based artist and writer. He received his Bachelor of Fine Arts in Sculpture at the Minneapolis College of Art and Design, practiced Studio Art at The Burren College of Art in Ireland, apprenticed for Atelier Van Lieshout in Rotterdam, The Netherlands, received a degree in Chinese Language Studies from the Communication University of China while helping develop the Rainbow School of Art, and was taught Tok Pisin by the Sawiyano Tribe of Papua New Guinea. He is currently managing the Sculpture Lab at the Milwaukee Institute of Art and Design. He has a passion to create opportunities for others, and is a strong advocate for the arts, children, education, and traveling to new places. Soft Feet is one of many checkpoints, as the author continues to write and travel daily.

www.ingramcontent.com/pod-product-compliance
Lightning Source LLC
Chambersburg PA
CBHW021156020426
42331CB00003B/88